Boost your
memory

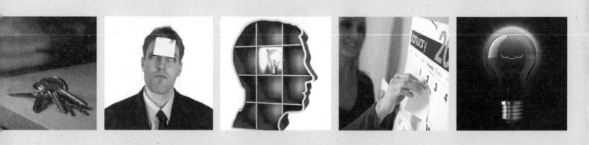

Boost your memory

Brilliant ideas you won't forget

Darren Bridger

brilliantideas

CAREFUL NOW

Most people have great memories, they just don't know it. This book can help you discover the power of your memory, but don't expect to turn into Marvo the Magnificent Memory Man overnight – and neither the author nor the publisher can be held responsible if you suddenly remember the awful incident of the family reunion, the spiked punch and great-aunt Gertie's hat.

Now there are some people who do have genuine medical reasons for poor memory; if you think this might be you, then do seek medical advice. Otherwise, find a pack of cards...

Acknowledgements

Thanks to Adam Field, Caterina Abreu, Melissa Haveman, David Lewis, Sophie Brown, James Wills, Katherine Hieronymus, Rebecca Clare and all the staff at Infinite Ideas who worked on the book.

First published in 2008 by
Infinite Ideas Limited
36 St Giles
Oxford, OX1 3LD
United Kingdom
www.infideas.com

A CIP catalogue record for this book is available from the British Library

ISBN 978-1-905940-62-2

Brand and product names are trademarks or registered trademarks of their respective owners.

Designed and typeset by Baseline Arts Ltd, Oxford
Printed in India

Brilliant ideas

Brilliant features

Each chapter of this book is designed to provide you with an inspirational idea that you can read quickly and put into practice straight away.

Throughout you'll find three features that will help you get right to the heart of the idea:

- *Here's an idea for you* Take it on board and give it a go – right here, right now. Get an idea of how well you're doing so far.

- *Defining idea* Words of wisdom from masters and mistresses of the art, plus some interesting hangers-on.

- *How did it go?* If at first you do succeed, try to hide your amazement. If, on the other hand, you don't, then this is where you'll find a Q and A that highlights common problems and how to get over them.

Introduction

Do you want to stop forgetting people's faces, appointments, crucial information for work and other vital facts? Far from being just one of many functions of the brain, memory is *the* most important skill we possess. Without memory, we'd lose our identity, as the cruelty of Alzheimer's disease shows. Without memory we would lose our ability to think. And without memory we would lose our ability to relate, work and bond with others.

Boost your memory puts a host of practical memory-enhancing ideas in your hands. Some of the following Ideas will teach you basic memory-boosting skills, some will suggest ways you can put those skills to work and some will lift the lid on the latest scientific findings about how to improve and protect memory.

There are a lot of myths and confusing ideas circulating about memory. What may seem obvious, or common sense, is not necessarily so. In this book I hope to help you separate fact from fantasy, and reveal the best techniques for you to use. Photographic memory, recovered memories, training your brain (like you'd work a muscle) to make it stronger, and popping pills to boost your brain are all popular ideas which have far less clear-cut evidence to support them than you might think.

In contrast, people overlook the very real benefits to your memory that come from healthy living: a balanced diet, regular exercise and enough sleep (even the odd daytime nap, if you can manage it). Equally, being well organised and focusing your attention are far more powerful memory techniques than you might think. All this will be covered later.

Ironically, some of the most powerful techniques for boosting your memory are also the oldest. Under the umbrella term 'Mnemonics' (it has a silent 'M'), these involve tapping into the fact that our brains have evolved to deal very well with both visual images and spatial locations. By turning facts into mental images, and imagining them along a route of locations, you can harness these natural memory powers to remember almost anything you like. The more improbable and emotionally charged the images the better, as our brains evolved to pay special attention to those features. Another part of your imagination that can boost your memory is your musical sense. Rhythm and rhyme are potent memory boosters. This explains why you might find it hard to remember the periodic table of elements, yet your memory banks are overflowing with old ad jingles!

Finally, for those after truly weapons-grade memory tools, investing time learning how to turn numbers into images will yield real returns in your ability to hold on to information. Like physical locations, we've already memorised the structure of numbers, making it another perfect candidate for natural memory harnessing.

In the Internet age, the demands on our memory are changing, and will continue to do so as technology advances exponentially. We can increasingly rely on being able to access information 'at our fingertips' ever more quickly and conveniently. Indeed, as computer memory drops in price and increases in power we'll have 'life recorder' devices which we can wear that will constantly write an audio-visual record of our day-by-day life. Add in sophisticated search software and we could have no need to ever again search our memories to recall events from our past; they will all be there in digital, high-definition glory.

'Why bother memorising information,' you may equally ask, 'if I can just look it up on the Internet instantly?' It's a good question, and sometimes it may *not* be worth memorising those things you can easily access by other means. Evidence is already showing that younger people are memorising fewer basic facts than previous generations did. A similar shift in memory occurred hundreds of years ago, as writing and then the printing press negated the need for people to memorise entire books (something we can now barely imagine doing!).

However, understanding how to improve your memory can improve your quality of life. Being able to carry information around in your head, rather than in a notebook or external organiser, will enrich your intelligence, not to mention your career and your social interactions. Also, the more information you know about a particular subject the more you are able to learn. It's a virtuous cycle. Equally, building your memory powers can make you more creative. If you've ever browsed around a library, you've probably had the experience of pleasantly stumbling upon useful information that you weren't looking for, but which turns out to link with what you were hunting. Similarly, if you don't have a well-stocked mental library, you're less likely to make creative connections between new information and old.

Understanding how and when to use your memory has never been more important. And with recent advances in scientific research on memory in the last couple of decades, we've never known so much about the brain – knowledge that you can now use to boost your memory, no matter how good or bad it currently is. So, whether you wish to improve your memory to boost your educational grades, widen your career opportunities, protect your ageing brain (or that of a relative) or simply enjoy getting more out of your mind, I hope you find this book useful.

1

So how much can you remember?

In what areas do you need to improve your memory? Well, let's find out!

Don't panic! Yes, this is a test, but I'm not trying to catch you out, there are no trick questions. Rather, the aim is to see where, and how, you can improve your memory.

The following test is by no means comprehensive, but is designed to just give you a rough idea of which area(s) you may need to spend most time on. For each question, just put a '1' in the relevant box.

Part A	Rarely	Sometimes	Often
How often do you forget people's names?	☐	☐	☐
How often do you forget your own personal numbers, such as your car registration or phone number?	☐	☐	☐
How often do you have problems remembering information for your job?	☐	☐	☐

	Rarely	Sometimes	Often
Do you usually find you can't remember jokes?	☐	☐	☐
Do you find it difficult to remember information when you are supposed to be learning new things?	☐	☐	☐
Totals	☐	☐	☐

Part B	Rarely	Sometimes	Often
Do you often forget where you've parked your car?	☐	☐	☐
Do you often lose things around the house?	☐	☐	☐
Do you find it hard to concentrate when trying to learn something new?	☐	☐	☐
Do you have weeks when you do no exercise (defined as a continuous thirty-minute session where your heart rate is taken above normal)?	☐	☐	☐
Are you typically disorganised?	☐	☐	☐
Totals	☐	☐	☐

Part C	Disagree	Agree somewhat	Agree
I have a worse than average memory	☐	☐	☐
Memory inevitably gets significantly worse with age	☐	☐	☐
I have a bad memory	☐	☐	☐
My memory isn't as good as I'd like it to be	☐	☐	☐
I wasn't born with a good memory	☐	☐	☐
Totals	☐	☐	☐

Scoring:
Total up the three columns of boxes in part A, then multiply the 'sometimes' total by two, and the 'often' total by three. Then add up the totals to give you a grand total for the whole of the part. Repeat for parts B and C.

As you've probably guessed, the three parts were testing three different things. If you got a high (ten plus) score on part A, then it would be wise to develop your memory strategies. These are the different techniques you can use

Be aware that we all have different strengths in learning new information. Some people prefer to study by listening, others by reading, writing, hearing themselves speak, or doing (such as building models or operating a piece of equipment). By becoming aware of your preferred method(s) of learning, you can choose to learn more in that way.

Here's an idea for you...

The advantage of a bad memory is that one enjoys several times the same good things for the first time.
FRIEDRICH NIETZSCHE

to increase your ability to remember. Most of the memory strategies revolve around two concepts. The first is tying the items to be remembered to a structure that's already in your memory, such as a location or journey that you know well or a number list. The second involves using your imagination and, in particular, creating incongruent and emotive imagery of the information you are trying to memorise.

If you got a similarly high score on part B, then it would be wise to examine your behaviour in relation to your memory. Although our memories are stored in our brains, our brains are dependent on our bodies and environment for good functioning. This might include increasing your attention; keeping healthy with enough sleep, a good diet, regular exercise and moderate sugar/caffeine consumption; being organised and writing good notes when appropriate.

Finally, if you got a high score on part C, then you might want to improve your attitude and self-beliefs about memory. The fact is that virtually everyone has a very good memory, one that works more often than it fails. Most memory masters say that everyone has a good enough natural memory to train it to great heights. Believing that you have a bad memory can become a self-fulfilling prophecy so, from now on, please banish that phrase from your lips!

Q **I got a low score on one/two/all three. What would you advise me to do?**

A *If you got a low score on one or more of the parts, then it just means that this area is not so much of a problem for you. But there is always room for improvement. Just start by improving the area you got the highest score on, or feel most motivation to improve.*

Q **How do I know if I, or a friend or relative, has a serious memory problem?**

A *The test was meant to give some pointers for memory improvements. While some of us think we have a 'bad' memory, there are others who genuinely do have a medical reason for poor memory performance. If you think this is the case with you, or someone you know, then it's better to be safe than sorry: seek a check-up from your doctor. There are two rules of thumb for needing to do this – if you regularly have trouble remembering even very basic, everyday information, and if you are experiencing other health or mental functioning problems.*

How did it go?

2

Let's get up to date

A quick tour through the latest scientific findings on memory.

Over the last couple of decades we've learned more about the workings of the brain than in all of previous history.

Great progress has been made, including some surprising findings. Keeping in mind that science is constantly moving, and future findings could overturn or revise what we currently know, here are what neuroscientists currently think about some of the most common beliefs about memory.

Growing new brain cells

Popular wisdom: You're born with as many brain cells as you'll ever have, and they slowly die out through life.

- The evidence: New research has shown that we can, in fact, grow new brain cells throughout life. This came as a big surprise to many neuroscientists. What this means is that as we age, our brains can continue to develop and learn.
- Advice: Continue learning throughout your life, and realise your memory doesn't have to decline as much as you might have previously thought.

Where are memories stored in the brain?

Popular wisdom: There is a memory store within the brain.

- The evidence: While there are a couple of structures within the brain which are

Here's an idea for you... **Stop telling yourself that you have a bad memory. Research shows that although memory abilities can decline naturally with age, it's not always as inevitable or as bad as we may think. Furthermore, the expectation that they will makes this worse! Catch yourself next time you are about to say you have a terrible memory.**

responsible for 'writing' our long term memories, they are not all stored within a single part. The hippocampi – two seahorse-shaped structures deep inside your brain, on either side, about level with your temples – are responsible for laying down many long-term memories, particularly those memories for facts and events that you are able to describe. The cerebellum, at the back of your brain (which contains more than half the neurons in the brain), is responsible for laying down memories for physical skills. However, neither of these structures actually holds the memories; these are mostly stored in the cerebral cortex. This is the six-layered outer/top part of the brain, which is most recent in evolutionary terms. Memories are probably stored in many areas of the cortex.

■ Advice: When trying to recall a forgotten piece of information, attempt to bring to mind as great a variety of details about it as possible: its appearance, texture, location, sound, meanings, etc. As memories are stored across your brain, any one of these varied associations could easily trigger it.

Do we all have photographic memory abilities, if only we could unlock them?
Popular wisdom: Everything which happens to us is stored somewhere in the brain, if only we could access it.

■ The evidence: Most neuroscientists would say that this is a myth. It wouldn't make sense for us to remember everything; most things we experience are not essential. Equally, it doesn't fit in with how we think memories are formed. However, people do exist who seem to be able to remember almost everything. It may be that such people have physically different brain wiring to most of us, meaning that while a human brain is, technically, capable of remembering almost everything, most people's brains are not. Most memory champions don't actually remember everything, but use memory strategies to remember specific things. Nevertheless, how memories are stored in the brain is still not fully understood and it may be possible that we store, if not everything, then far more than we currently think.

If the brain were so simple we could understand it, we would be so simple we couldn't.

LYALL WATSON, biologist and author

Defining idea...

- Advice: Don't set unrealistic expectations for developing a photographic memory. Instead, concentrate on improving your memory by looking after your health and learning memory-boosting techniques.

Can we recover suppressed memories from childhood?

Popular wisdom: Certain memories, particularly traumatic ones, from our childhood become hidden or blocked, and can be recovered by a therapist using techniques like hypnosis.

- The evidence: While this may be possible, psychologists are a lot more sceptical about this than they were a decade or two ago. We now know that it's quite common for people to generate 'memories' of events that never happened. Every act of remembering is, in a sense, partially aided by our imagination as we reconstruct events. When a person is being guided by a therapist to recall a supposed suppressed memory, they can be vulnerable to being led to construct a false memory which is either a distortion or confusion of events, or, indeed, the creation of an event which never occurred.

- Advice: Not everything you think you remember, particularly from a long time ago, necessarily happened the way you think it did. If you are uncertain, and are unable to corroborate a memory with other people or facts, treat it sceptically.

What is déjà vu?

Popular wisdom: Sometimes you have the sensation that you've experienced something before.

■ The evidence: Everyone agrees that this phenomenon exists, but there is less certainty as to what causes it. One theory is that the information is processed by your memory milliseconds before you become consciously aware of it. While information usually enters your short-term memory first, déjà vu could be the rare occasion when information somehow jumps straight into your long-term memory instead – then when you come to consciously process it you have the feeling that you already know it. Another explanation is that you've experienced something very similar before, which you erroneously believe was the same.

■ Advice: Wonder at the mystery of your mind and remember that there are still many things we don't fully understand about memory!

How did it go?

Q   I've heard that listening to classical music can boost brain power. Would this work with memory too?

A   Sadly, this turns out to be a myth. However, musical training can improve brain power, so learning to play a musical instrument could have some secondary benefits for your memory.

Q   I've heard that we only use 10% of our brains. Is this true?

A   No. We're constantly using all parts of our brains. However, most of us are probably often only operating at a fraction of our memory's potential.

3

Close your eyes and visualise

Making pictures in your mind is probably the single most vital memory trick. Here's how to boost your ability to visualise.

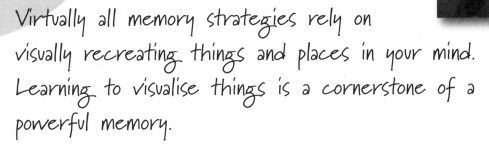

Virtually all memory strategies rely on visually recreating things and places in your mind. Learning to visualise things is a cornerstone of a powerful memory.

It's no surprise that great geniuses are often called 'visionaries': a highly developed visual imagination seems to be present in many of history's greatest thinkers. In particular, those with the most powerful memory abilities virtually always use their visual imagination to aid in memorising. Most of the effective techniques for memorising large quantities of information are based on visualising. For example, a young British man called Daniel Tammet is able to learn a new language in one week by turning words into shapes, colours and textures. Not all of us can hope to match this level of skill, but we can all improve our memorisation powers through using visual imagery.

We are very visual creatures; apart from sound, no other sense dominates our thinking and mental functions so much. Our brains have evolved to work well with images and, in a sense, images are the natural language of the mind.

Here's an idea for you...

Try your hand at drawing. It's a great way to increase your ability to visualise. Even if you think you're bad at drawing, you can soon improve through practice. Anyway, the aim is not to become the next da Vinci, but to increase your awareness of your visual sense. Start by placing an object in front of you, look at it and absorb as many details as you can. Then look away and try to sketch it. Then look back and compare your sketch with the object; note any details you missed.

There are some exercises that can help you to increase your ability to visualise. One technique is to look at an object, then very briefly close your eyes, for not much longer than a blink, and try to see it in your mind's eye. If you are having trouble seeing it, open your eyes and stare at it some more, then close your eyes again. Keep repeating this until you start to be able to see at least a ghostly outline of it with your eyes closed. Another technique you might like to try is to relax somewhere and close your eyes, then describe out loud any images you see, no matter how wispy or brief they appear. The act of describing them out loud focuses your attention on them and should, with practice, help to increase the strength of the images.

The second aspect to using your visual imagination is turning ideas quickly into images. This is particularly important when the ideas are more abstract and require some imagination applied before they can be translated into something more tangible. For example, how do you visualise the concept of 'courage'? You may think of a soldier running into battle, or perhaps the cowardly lion from *The Wizard of Oz* who went in search of his courage. The important thing when you're doing this is not to think of the most 'clever' image, but the one which comes to mind first, and is strongest for you. That will be the one you're most likely to remember. When you get good at this, you'll realise that it's possible to express complex ideas in relatively simple images. A picture, as they say, really can be worth a thousand words.

Your visual images don't have to be photorealistic. Often this is an unachievable goal for most of us, anyway. As long as you can bring the general concept of what the thing looks like to mind, that will be good enough. You may find that you typically just get a brief snatch of the image appearing, and that's enough to let you know what the whole image is. Equally, your images don't have to be true to life; in fact, it helps to make them larger than life. Making your images funny, larger or smaller than reality, emotional or otherwise dramatic and vivid will make them more memorable. Don't be afraid to go wild with your images: only you will see them!

Imagination is more important than knowledge. Knowledge is limited. Imagination encircles the world.
ALBERT EINSTEIN

Defining idea...

How did it go?

Q **I'm still having trouble in visualising anything when my eyes are closed, is there anything else you can suggest?**

A *Another way to stimulate your ability to see images in your 'mind's eye' is to close your eyes while facing a light source, ideally either quite bright (such as sitting outside on a sunny day), or flickering (such as sitting in front of a fireplace or a burning candle). This will create movement and shapes on the inside of your eyelids, which will stimulate your mind into forming mental imagery. Also, you could try gently rubbing your closed eyelids. This will generate spots of light, called phosphemes, which can easily evoke mental imagery. Remember also that your images don't have to be photographically perfect, just good enough to get the general idea across.*

Q **I find it very difficult to translate certain ideas into visual images. Can you help?**

A *This is an ability which will strengthen with practice. Many people also feel inhibited in doing this because they think their images are silly. So just remind yourself that no one else needs to know what your images are; they are safe within the privacy of your own mind! To stimulate your imagination, use the following questions to help turn any idea into an image. How would your idea be displayed as a street sign? How would a cartoonist illustrate the idea? What does the idea sound like? What actions does it imply? What profession is it most linked to? What colour is it most like? What animal does it resemble?*

4

Spaces and places

Tap into your brain's amazing memory for places in order to remember anything.

Pay attention, this is the mother of (nearly) all memory enhancement methods. It starts from the fact that while you might lose a kitchen utensil, you never lose the kitchen.

Fixed locations, such as familiar buildings and landscapes, are generally easy to recall. Not only do their details spring to mind easily, but they are highly structured – the two perfect ingredients for a system to store information. In fact, our brains seem to specialise in being good at learning locations. For example, the parts of the brain that deal most with memorising, the hippocampi, are also the parts which deal with spatial locations. In fact, London taxi drivers – who memorise thousands of locations and routes – have been found to have larger than average hippocampi. The same is even true for rats trained to memorise mazes!

The ancient Greeks and Romans knew about this method of memorising, and used it to learn long speeches. The father of memory-improvement methods – a Greek poet called Simonides, who lived about 2500 years ago – was said to have first discovered this technique. A banqueting hall (in which he'd just recited a poem)

Here's an idea for you...

Dig out some photos of the place you are going to use, or, better still, go and take a walk around it (if possible). Try to notice as many details about it as you can. What are the unique features of each area of your location? Use all your senses. Study each area of the location until you know it inside out. Putting the preparation work in at this stage will pay off when you need to memorise something quickly.

had collapsed, leaving all the dinner guests crushed beyond recognition. The next day Simonides was able to recall the names of all the guests, just by mentally walking around the banquet table, recalling who was sitting at which point. From then onwards, Simonides used this method of 'loci' – or locations – to remember his poetry.

To make this method work, all you need to do is choose a location with lots of visual features with which to associate your pieces of information, like a spatial filing cabinet that you can walk around in your imagination. For example, if you have to remember ten items for a shopping list, simply think of ten locations around your home. These could be rooms, or pieces of furniture, which are then individually associated with each item on your list. When you get to the supermarket, just mentally walk through this route around your house and each item should easily pop into your mind.

To take a more advanced example: think back to your old school. Even if it's been years since you attended it, the chances are good that you can still remember the basic layout of the buildings, and you may even be able to remember quite a bit of detail about the individual rooms. Take a moment and think back to it. Imagine walking into the main entrance, and trace a route around the buildings until you've covered as many rooms as you can remember. Aim for as much detail as you can possibly recall. You'll probably surprise yourself with how much you can remember.

Now, how many rooms could you recall? And how many areas within each room (the blackboards, the windows, the cupboards, etc.) could you recall? You may even find that a few details that you hadn't thought about in years come back into your mind. Amazing how much information can be locked away in those little grey cells, isn't it? Each one of those rooms and areas within rooms is a potential 'hook' on which to attach another memorable image. Just turn the thing you wish to remember into a vivid image and associate it with your location image.

Once your places are all fixed in order, then you can walk through the door and make your start. If you are going to use a great many images, then let the buildings be hundreds or thousands of units in extent; if you only want a few, then take a single reception hall and just divide it up by its corners.
MATTEO RICCI, Italian memory expert (1552–1610)

Defining idea...

You can even use mental locations to create different 'themed' areas. For example, you could use the mental image of your school library to remember information about books you want to read, the home economics classroom to remember shopping lists, and the playground to remember the names of people you meet. You may want to reserve some locations for permanent memories (e.g. facts you wish to store) and some for more short-term memories, like shopping lists.

You can increase your repertoire of locations to give yourself more mental storage space. In fact, there's probably no limit to how much you can memorise using this system. Usually, with most things, the more details you have to remember, the harder it gets. But when it comes to spaces and places, the more details you have, the easier it becomes to remember them.

How did it go?

Q **I just can't visualise the place, even though I know it well. Is that vital?**

A *Although it's best to be able to actually visualise the place in your mind's eye, this isn't strictly essential. As long as you can easily recall the details of the location, that should be enough.*

Q **I'm finding it difficult to remember the order of the locations; I sometimes even miss one or two out! What can I do?**

A *Try adding in a marker image at every fifth position along your route. Alternatively, is the reason you're having trouble with remembering the order because you keep thinking of a different order? If so, simply adopt that order instead. The aim here is to create a system that is easily memorable, not to just challenge oneself to remember one that is difficult.*

5

When not to remember

Why perfect recall is not necessarily best.

Wouldn't it be great to have a photographic memory? Imagine: take one brief look at something, and — click! — you would have an instant, perfect record of it.

You could then go back through your memories and recall any detail, no matter how small.

This may sound fantastic, but we do know that the human brain is capable of this. The bad news is that it seems to only occur in people with some structural abnormality to the brain. Memory techniques that anyone can learn can massively boost your memory power but only those born different, or who develop some major brain difference through accident or otherwise, can attain this level of memory skill.

A small number of people who have autism also seem to have something approaching a photographic memory. The most famous example is the American, Kim Peek, who was the inspiration for the character played by Dustin Hoffman in the film *Rainman*. Kim has memorised almost 12,000 books, and only takes eight to

Here's an idea for you...

Make a list of information that is better memorised than stored in written or electronic form. For example, while it might be nice to memorise all your friends' and family's phone numbers, in the real world, where we all have limited time and attention, this might not be the best use of your memorising efforts.

ten seconds to read and memorise each page. Another autistic memory master is Stephen Wiltshire. He can look at a city view once, then produce, entirely from memory, an astonishingly detailed and accurate drawing of it. Other people have been born with no obvious mental impairments (such as autism) but with an automatic tendency to memorise almost all the details of their everyday lives. One woman, identified in the research literature only as 'AJ', developed a powerful obsession with remembering everything after a childhood relocation gave her a strong emotional need to hold on to the past. However, she may have been born with this ability, as she claims that she doesn't consciously spend time memorising things. Mention any date in her past, and she can recall, with ease and in detail, what she did that day.

However, such high-powered memories come at a price. AJ sees her extraordinary memory as a curse, not a gift. 'I remember good,' she says, 'but I also remember bad – and every bad choice, and I really don't give myself a break. Your memory is the way it is to protect you. I feel like it just hasn't protected me. I would love just for five minutes to be a simple person and not have all this stuff in my head. Most people have called what I have a gift,' she adds, 'but I call it a burden.' This highlights the benefit of not thinking too much about negative experiences.

As well as the emotional downsides of a perfect memory, there can also be a loss of ability to get the 'gist' of something. When you remember everything, you take everything literally. This seems to mitigate against summarising information in a meaningful, but abstract and fuzzy way. One man called Shereshevshy, who (like AJ) remembered everything that had ever happened to him, had an inability to recognise faces as their details were constantly changing. Faces are always seen in different lighting conditions, angles, etc., and with different expressions. To a literal mind, they can become impossible to recognise. Total recall seems to prevent understanding subtle meanings and metaphors. It is a very literal way to perceive the world. So, while a photographic memory sounds good in theory, the reality is that most of us wouldn't want it.

Forgetting prevents the shear mass of life's detail from critically slowing down the retrieval of relevant experience and so impairing the mind's ability to abstract, infer and learn.
GERD GIGERENZER, psychologist

Defining idea...

Another reason why we wouldn't want to remember everything is that it isn't necessary. For almost all of human history, right up until the invention of the printing press, the only way most people could have information at their fingertips was to memorise it. In the past, memory was even more vital than it is now. Today we not only have books and widespread literacy, but all manner of ways to store and retrieve information electronically. The Internet, mobile phones (with their own memories for phone numbers) and digital personal organisers have become our external memories, relieving our brains of the pressure to memorise all our essential information.

Recent research has shown that younger people are now significantly less likely than older people to remember basic personal information, such as birth dates of relatives or even their own phone numbers. This, it seems, is not a function of age but a cultural change, brought on by an increasing reliance on these external digital devices. Why bother spending time and effort memorising facts that can be instantly accessed on your phone or computer?

How did it go?

Q I'm not sure I follow the problem about not recognising faces. Can you give me another example?

A   Well, for example, think about reading a novel. What is important to us is to understand the overall meaning and the journeys of the characters, rather than to be able to just regurgitate it word for word.

Q I tend to go over bad memories in my mind. I've heard that this can be therapeutic, but is it?

A   The 'talking cure' model of psychotherapy has mixed-to-weak evidence to back up its benefit. Certainly, if you have worries, it can be helpful to talk them over with a friend or a loved one, a problem shared can be a problem halved. Equally, if you are suffering from a serious psychological problem, you should seek treatment. However, you may want to think twice before embarking on a never-ending or long-term course of psychotherapy.

6
Remember a list of eleven items

Need to remember a to-do list, or a list of items you need to buy?

Here's one of the most basic memory skills: how to quickly remember a short list of any items.

In everyday life it's very handy to be able to store such simple lists in our memory. This is one of the best methods.

One of the things you can already remember with ease is how to count to ten. By piggy-backing on this memory structure that already exists within your brain, you can easily remember any list of items. There are two versions, both of which are going to apply the powers of your imagination to this pre-existing structure of numbers. Use either, depending on which you prefer, or feel free to use both.

The first system involves creating mental images for things which rhyme with each number. I've provided an example list here, with more than one different option for most of the numbers. Simply choose the word which you are most likely to remember and find the easiest to visualise. The word that you choose should immediately trigger a vivid mental image. It shouldn't be something abstract. Ideally it should be a noun, a 'thing'.

Here's an idea for you...

Productivity experts recommend that you make your to-do items as specific as possible. Rather than just write, for example, 'contact Bill', specify how you will contact him: 'phone Bill' or 'email Bill'. Take as many of the decisions about a task at the beginning when you are writing them down, and you will make it easier to complete your to-do list, as less decision making will be needed to get through it.

Number	Rhyming word
zero	hero (such as a superhero)
one	gun, bun, sun
two	shoe, crew, ewe, zoo
three	tree, ski, pee
four	door, drawer
five	hive (beehive), dive
six	sticks, bricks
seven	heaven
eight	gate, crate, plate
nine	wine, sign (road sign)
ten	den, hen, pen

Go through the list and decide upon one word only for each number. If English isn't your first language, or if you don't like any of my choices, feel free to select your own words. Then make sure you can easily recall the image for each number. Make your mental image as bold, dramatic and emotion-laden as possible. Run through the list a few times and test yourself. If you are having any problems remembering any of the images, try another one, or try adjusting the image to make it more memorable. The most important thing is that the image should come to mind almost automatically when you think of the number.

Now, in order to memorise anything, you will attach each thing to be memorised to one of the numbers (typically you would want to start from zero). You attach them by creating a vivid mental image which combines the item with the image for the number. For example, if you were memorising a shopping list, and your first item was 'milk', you might imagine Superman (a hero) gulping down a large carton of milk. Or, even better,

Superman holding up a cow and drinking the milk straight from the udder! The second image is better because it's bizarre and potentially humorous – making it more likely you'll remember it.

Memory is the diary that we all carry with us.
OSCAR WILDE

Defining idea...

Alternatively, you can use this second number system, which is based on words which look like each of the figures.

Number	Similar-looking object
0	sun
1	pen/pencil/candle
2	swan
3	handcuffs
4	sailing boat
5	curtain hook
6	elephant's trunk
7	boomerang
8	snowman
9	balloon on a string
10	bat and ball / knife and plate

You may even find this system simpler; as it is already visually based, it doesn't require you to translate the sound of a word into an image. The image is already there. Just as before, you then simply make a mental image of each word to use as your memory 'hook' on which to hang your pieces of information.

The limitations to the system are that it's not ideal on its own for storing large quantities of information. You could, in theory, extend it to cover the numbers from eleven to twenty. This would probably be easier using the visual system than the rhyming system. Also, once you've mastered other systems for remembering information, you'll find your own ways of combining them with this method.

How did it go?

Q **Whenever I plan my to-do or shopping lists, I just write them down on paper. Is there any other way this system could be of benefit to me?**

A *Sometimes great ideas strike when you are unable to write them down, such as when you are driving or walking the dog. This system is perfect as an internal notebook for keeping track of such ideas until you get back in front of your actual notebook.*

Q **If I use this system regularly, how can I avoid getting old lists confused with new ones?**

A *This is a danger, although there are ways to minimise it. Firstly if you are using it for shopping lists, you may just like to create a timeless list of essentials which you always need, or would always wish to run through in your mind when you're at the shops. That way the list always stays the same. Secondly, you could use the shape system for one area of life (shopping lists) and the rhyme system for another (capturing ideas). Also, these systems are best for holding information for just a few hours. So if you don't constantly rehearse your images beyond that time, you'll probably forget them anyway.*

7

Faces and names

Your memory can save you from the hell of social embarrassment. Here's how to never forget another person's name.

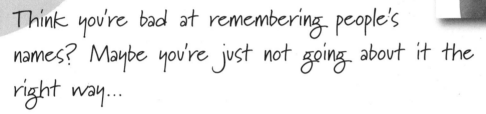

Think you're bad at remembering people's names? Maybe you're just not going about it the right way...

We're sometimes unable to recognise people we've met, let alone recall their name. Most people take this as a sign that they have a bad memory. But this is probably not the case. Names can be a particularly hard thing to remember. For one thing, they are abstract and unconnected to the person; while Mr Baker used to be a baker, today his name is not related to his profession. For another, we usually hear names only once when a person is introduced to us, and often we don't even hear the name properly, but smile and shake hands anyway. Something mundane, like a name, which is only encountered once, is unlikely to be encoded into a strong memory. Finally, the worst possible scenario is being introduced to a large group of people at once. Any more than seven people at the same time and your short-term memory will be overloaded. Then there's almost no chance you'll remember them.

So, if you often find you forget names, just understand that it's not something that comes automatically. To be good at it you're going to have to put a little bit of effort in.

Here's an idea for you...

Business cards can be a great tool for helping you to remember names. If you regularly meet people in a business setting, always keep a stack with you. They can obviously even be handed out in non-business settings, but in those situations you're less likely to get one in return. When someone does give you a business card, write on the back as soon as possible where you met them, and any details which will help you remember them or their face. This will then help you when you come to review their name in the future to strengthen the memory. Also, why not help others to remember your face by putting a portrait photo of yourself on your own business card?

Use the N.A.M.E. acronym to remember how to store names.

Notice

If the information doesn't go in properly at first, you're not going to be able to store and recall it. Listen carefully to the person's name when it's first mentioned, and pay careful attention to their face. Make a quick check of the following: hair colour, eye colour, skin tone and bone structure. Pay attention to any striking facial features. This can all be quite tricky at first, when you are having to divide your attention between noticing these features and also talking to the person without appearing as though you are staring at their face.

Ask

Ask them to repeat their name if you didn't hear it clearly, or to clarify how it's spelled. This is not only useful in making sure you get their name correctly, but it provides another repetition to strengthen the memory.

Therefore, even if you did hear the name correctly, it can't do any harm to ask them to clarify it! Also, you could ask about any unusual names; for example, you could ask which country an unusual-sounding name originally came from.

Mention

Mention the person's name back to them a couple of times during conversation. You'll need to use your own judgement on this, as mentioning a name too many times can come across as a bit odd or too ingratiating! The key point is that new information is most vulnerable to being forgotten in the early stages, so any repetitions of the name in the minutes after you've heard it are valuable. Done discretely, it can't do any harm; most people love hearing their own name mentioned, so the very act of echoing it back to them a few times will help them warm to you!

I never forget a face, but in your case I'll make an exception.
GROUCHO MARX

Defining idea...

Envisage

Use your imagination to create a visual link between the person's name and their face or something about them. There are a couple of ways to do this. Firstly, you could associate the person with someone of the same name you already know, either personally or someone famous. Secondly, you could turn their name itself into an image. Sometimes this is easy. For example, names like Elizabeth Firth (sounds like Elizabeth the First, which would evoke an image of the famous queen), or Bill Sacks (evokes an image of a large sack of unpaid bills?) may naturally lend themselves to visualisation. Where this is not possible, you may need to break the name up into elements. For example, then name Christopher Ashton may evoke the images of Christ and a town ('ton' sounds like 'town') covered in ash.

Finally, never guess a name. Not only will it seem rude if you get it wrong, it could almost mean that next time you meet that person, you remember your previous wrong guess rather than their actual name. Instead, if you really can't remember it, ask them politely.

How did it go?

Q **How can I remember someone's name if I can't see their face – for instance, if I first talk to them on the phone?**

A *This makes it far easier as you can write down the name straightaway. Rather than associate it with their face, you could then associate it with their voice (accents and voice intonations are easier to concentrate on when talking to someone on the phone).*

Q **The process of turning a name into a visual image is pretty complex and I find this too hard and time consuming when I'm meeting someone new. What can I do?**

A *This is very much an art, and it gets easier and quicker the more you do it. Practice will help you speed up and turn it into a habit. Rehearse with names in the phone book, or whenever you meet people whose names you'll find out, but who you are not under pressure to remember, such as shop assistants (just glance at their name badges).*

8

Healthy body, healthy memory

Get up from in front of the TV, and you could improve your memory.

Your brain doesn't operate in total isolation from your body. Taking regular exercise and avoiding getting overweight could help boost your memory as well as your physical health.

In today's wealthy Western societies, many of us are more sedentary than we evolved to be. Our bodies evolved on the East African plains, at a time when we would be on our feet for much of the day, hunting or gathering food. We developed to crave sugary and fatty foods – good sources of energy – and these were scarce. The car, the office cubicle and the easy chair were still far in the future. Today, with cheap transportation, abundant fatty and sugary foods and very few people doing physically demanding jobs, it's easier than ever to become physically out of shape. But inactivity can be bad for your brain and, in particular, your memory. And this is especially true the older you are.

Here's an idea for you...

Get hold of a pedometer. These are small devices which measure how many steps you've taken. Try wearing it each day, and whenever possible, try taking the stairs rather than the lift, and try walking rather than driving. Keep a daily or weekly record of how many steps you've taken, and aim to constantly improve it. You could even get competitive and ask a friend to wear one too!

Moderate cardiovascular exercise has been found to improve memory abilities, and ward off the development of dementia. The key is that the exercise session needs to be at least thirty minutes long, and you should do it several times a week, ideally every day. This could be anything which gets your heart beating above its normal rate. Exercise such as swimming, cycling or even brisk walking is perfect for this. One study, for example, asked volunteers to go for a brisk, one-hour walk three times per week. After just three months of this exercise they had knocked three years of ageing off their brains, and doubled the amount of blood circulating through the brain, too. Integrating exercise into your weekly schedule could, therefore, be of great benefit to your ability to learn new information, and recall the information you already know. Exercise can also increase your memory powers by increasing alertness and clear thinking, reducing anxiety and depression and helping you to get a good night's sleep. The benefits accrue to both young and old. Studies have shown that children who exercise regularly are better able to concentrate on learning in school. Other studies have shown that older people taking regular exercise not only improve their memory skills but reduce their risk of developing Alzheimer's disease.

While our brains make up only 2% of our weight, they consume 20% of our energy. They are hungry for oxygen and glucose. This means they are dependent on good blood flow and good regulation of blood sugar. This is where exercise helps. Poor regulation of blood sugar, for example, is associated with smaller hippocampi – the brain regions responsible for laying down long-term memories. Regular exercise will increase the amount of blood flowing through your brain, and improve the delivery of blood sugar. This will help new neurons – brain cells – to grow. Until recently, scientists didn't think adults could grow new neurons; you just had to make do with what you were born with. But we can – and exercise helps this, as well as strengthening connections between existing neurons, improving long-term memories.

Losing weight will improve how you regulate your glucose, and we have shown that improved glucose regulation is associated with better memory.
DR ANTONIO CONVIT, New York University School of Medicine

Defining idea...

There is also growing evidence that obesity may itself impair memory abilities. A hormone called leptin, which helps us regulate our appetite, does not reach the brain so well in many obese people. Lack of this hormone in the brains of mice impaired their long-term memory and ability to learn.

However, we don't currently have a complete understanding of the benefits of exercise on memory and more research needs to be done. So far the evidence suggests that it's older people, particularly older women, who gain the most benefit to their memory from exercising. But it's possible that the effectiveness may indeed vary from person to person. Nevertheless, given the health benefits of exercise, what do you have to lose? Should you exercise regularly? It's a no-brainer!

How did it go?

Q **I tried to take up regular exercise but I couldn't keep it going for more than a couple of weeks. How can I keep up my exercising?**

A *The best way to ensure you'll exercise regularly is to pick a type of exercise that you enjoy. It's no good trying to force yourself into doing something that you resist, otherwise the chances are that you won't be doing it for long. It's well known that most people who join gyms do not keep up the regular visits they intended to. If you are self-conscious, for example, going to the gym may be too stressful for you to enjoy it, and a more solitary form of exercise might be better. Alternatively, if you find solitary exercise boring, then consider playing a team sport or finding an exercise partner.*

Q **How can I find time for exercising three times a week when my schedule is already full?**

A *Try adding little bits of physical activity into your daily movements. Could you walk or cycle to work rather than drive? Could you take a walk during your lunch breaks? Or take the stairs rather than use an escalator? Such micro exercise sessions can add up to significant benefits if you practice them regularly. It would still be best to work in more substantial exercise sessions during your week if you can.*

9

Work smart, not hard

Just practising can be a waste of time. It's strategies you need...

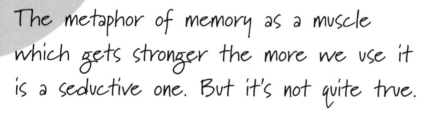

The metaphor of memory as a muscle which gets stronger the more we use it is a seductive one. But it's not quite true.

There have been a number of 'exercise your memory' video games and puzzles in recent years that have contributed to this idea's popularity. However, if you spent an hour a day memorising a poem, for example, this wouldn't help you in recalling the name of what's-her-face next time you bump into her in the shops. Though regular exercises can improve your physical health, the same is not quite true for your memory.

Memorising a range of information on one particular subject doesn't necessarily improve your memory in general. There are a couple of exceptions to this. Practising memorising information may improve your ability to concentrate, which may have a knock-on effect on your ability to memorise in general. Also, practising particular memory techniques can improve your proficiency at that technique. And practising memorising information about a subject will almost certainly increase your ability to learn more information about that subject. This is because you'll have more pieces of information with which to associate and understand new facts.

Here's an idea for you...

Whenever approaching a new area you wish to memorise, first look for how you can best structure it. Does it already have a natural structure? Is it linear (i.e. does one fact lead on to another in a straight progression) or does it have a whole range of areas which all branch off from the core facts? If you are learning a language, take time at the beginning to study its structure. This can unlock the code that makes learning it much easier.

Nevertheless, in general, the metaphor of memory as a muscle is unclear. However, simply by learning memory-boosting techniques, and becoming proficient with them, you can greatly improve your ability to memorise. Here are three additional ways you can improve your memory without exercising it.

Prioritise

Not all information is equally important to memorise. Some things are best stored in a diary, notepad, PDA or other device. Some information is best looked up as and when you need it. How do you decide what is worth learning and what isn't? Firstly, virtually all personal contact information, like addresses, phone numbers, email addresses, etc., are almost certainly best stored somewhere external to your brain. Secondly, if information has a short shelf life, then it's probably not worth memorising. If you are only likely to need certain information when in front of your computer, then it might be best to rely on search engines for it. The one exception to this is when you think having information readily accessible in your memory will help you think or understand new information better.

Create a system

If you can develop a system for recording information in an organised way, it lessens the burden on your memory. Develop a routine for where you place things. For example, create a 'central storage station' in your home for keeping important items. You may, in fact, want two: one for the things you take out with you a lot, such as wallet/purse, keys, coins, etc. (this one is best positioned near your front door) and another (positioned in a more secure place) for your most vital paperwork, such as your passport, birth certificate and so on. Keep a pad of sticky notes next to your phone. These are more versatile than an ordinary notepad, and can be placed in prominent positions to leave messages for others so you won't have to remember to tell them.

The chains of habit are too light to be felt until they are too strong to be broken.
ANON

Defining idea...

Use a 'thirty-day trial run' to create a new habit

The limited trial run is a method often used by businesses to get you hooked on their product. Trying something for a month is usually long enough to solidify it into a habit, and learning a habit subsequently takes the effort out of a behaviour. You don't have to invest so much conscious thought into performing the action.

Embarking on a new habit can be daunting, particularly if it involves giving up an already ingrained one. Deciding to do something for only a limited time period – like thirty days – takes the pressure off you, and makes you less apprehensive and therefore more likely to get started on it. You could also try making learning itself into a habit; for example, by spending at least half an hour each evening reading.

How did it go?

Q Does this mean it's pointless for me to use any memory-training games?

A *While I can't discount every single one, in general there is a lack of strong evidence that such games will boost your memory. There may be secondary benefits to using them, such as increasing your powers of concentration. There may also be an indirect benefit in that it may motivate you to pay more attention to your memory, which may in turn improve your memory. But there's no evidence that simply doing such exercises will help your ability to learn or recall other information.*

Q Are there no regular exercises I can do to boost my memory?

A *If you're trying to improve your memory for a particular thing, you may like to sometimes review everything you know in that area, to keep your memories for it strong. But you don't need to do this very often. Only once every few months, or even once a year, should do the trick. Another thing you might like to practise is your ability to quickly turn things to be remembered into visual images. This is really a strategy that can genuinely boost your memory, so if you can practise these imaginative skills, you will definitely benefit.*

10

Carroll's curious language of numbers

Turning numbers into letters, words or images is one of the cornerstones of memory techniques.

Numbers have their own order, but are hard to visualise; words are easy to visualise but lack order. However, if you combine them, you have a very powerful memory system.

Charles Lutwidge Dodgson is famous as a nineteenth-century mathematician and writer under the pseudonym of Lewis Carroll; he's probably best known for the topsy-turvy world of *Alice in Wonderland*. However, less well known was that he was also a talented poet. He developed a memory system called the 'Memoria Technica' which took memory techniques back to their poetic roots. It's similar to other number systems in that it converts numbers into words in order to make them more memorable, but his has the advanced addition of using rhyming couplets to further enhance your ability to remember the words.

Carroll was multilingual and his system translated numbers not only into English but also into other foreign languages. He gave each number two consonants to be associated with it, so that you have a bit of latitude in which you use. This is particularly useful when you have more than one of the same number to

Here's an idea for you...

Colours evoke feelings and associations in us, but so can numbers; it's just that we are not so aware of them. Take the numbers between one and nine and think about what each evokes within you. What is the primary feeling or sensation of the number? If it were a colour, person or sound, what would it be like? Becoming aware of these associations we have with numbers helps to make them more memorable.

remember, as it gives you some variety in how you construct your word.

First you need to put some work into remembering his number/letter code:

0 = Z or R   (ZeRo)

1 = B or C   (B and C are the first two consonants in the alphabet)

2 = D or W   (Duo and tWo)

3 = T or J   (Tres – Spanish – and J, simply because it was the only consonant left which hadn't been used!)

4 = F or Q   (Four and Quattuor – Latin)

5 = L or V   (in Roman numerals: L = 50 and V = 5)

6 = S or X   (SiX)

7 = P or M   (sePteM – Latin)

8 = H or K   (Huit – French – and oKto – Greek)

9 = N or G   (NiNe, and 9 also looks like a g)

Now, for any number, you will have a consonant; put them together, and a word will be suggested. All you need to do is add in the vowels. For example, 855 equals HLL, which can easily become HeLLo.

Carroll's system then involved making a rhyming couplet with the very last word representing the word to be remembered. As an example, Carroll used the date of 1492, the year in which Columbus discovered America. While everyone remembers the millennium in which this occurred, we can drop the 1 and just endeavour to remember the 492. The number 4 is associated with 'F', 9 with 'N' and 2 with 'D'.

FND can be turned into FouND, replicating the same 'trick' as in some other number systems: that words with their vowels taken out are still identifiable. 'The poetic faculty must now be brought into play,' wrote Carroll, 'and the following couplet will soon be evolved:
Columbus sailed the world around,
Until America was FouND.'

If possible, invent the couplets for yourself; you will remember them better than any others.
LEWIS CARROLL

Defining idea...

Another example he gave helped him remember the founding date of St John's College (1555):
'They must have a bevel
To keep them so LeVeL.'
The couplet refers to the college's famous flat lawns. This highlights another benefit of the system: the rhyming couplet can be about the thing you are trying to remember. This may seem a simple, obvious point, but it means that the couplet itself becomes easier to remember.

Of course, the complexity of this system means that you need a fair amount of time, not only to memorise the initial association of the consonants with each number, but to devise couplets for whatever numbers you are trying to memorise.

All this wasn't just a dry, theoretical exercise; Carroll regularly used the system to remember dates. In particular, when giving visitors tours of Oxford University, Carroll would use his system to remember the founding dates of the various colleges. Indeed, this is where Carroll's system works best: in remembering dates. Most things you need to remember dates for, such as historical events or birth dates, are easily turned into a couplet, and can be represented by three numbers (you can usually do without the '1'), which is the perfect size for turning into a word.

How did it go?

Q **This seems a lot of work just for remembering dates. Is there any other use for this number code?**

A *Yes! Firstly, you could use it to remember your bank account PIN number, or even a phone number (although in that instance you'll probably need to use two words rather than one). Also, this number code will work with other memory number systems (i.e. the Major and Dominic Systems).*

Q **I'm not much of a poet. Any more tips on how to come up with the couplets?**

A *When devising one, think about the single most memorable thing about your subject. It should be something which immediately pops into your mind, without any effort. Then make your couplet about that stand-out feature. Also, try injecting humour, exaggeration, surrealism or emotional content into your couplet, all of which will make it more memorable.*

11

Chunking

Organising items into groups makes them more memorable.

Your memory is a little bit like a filing system: the better organised it is, the easier it is to retrieve information.

One of the most versatile and powerful memory techniques is grouping or 'chunking' information down into smaller pieces. This technique is particularly valuable when you have a list of letters or numbers to remember.

The average person can only hold between seven and nine 'bits' of information in their consciousness at once (this is known as your digit span). But what if those bits were the file names for stores of lots of other bits of information? If you do that, then you've effectively got around the seven-to-nine rule, and managed to cram many more bits in. Whenever we think of something, other concepts are triggered, which then in turn trigger their own associated concepts. If you said 'humpty' – equivalent to one 'bit' of information – to a child, it could trigger the whole nursery rhyme of Humpty-dumpty, which, taken word by word, is actually twenty-six bits. Likewise one word can often be enough to trigger a whole pop song, prayer, poem or joke in your mind. So, you can also make information more memorable by simplifying it down into one or several trigger words which will provoke you to

Here's an idea for you...

Are you trying to learn a complex physical skill, like driving, touch-typing or a particular sport? Simply break the skill down into parts and master each part, before bringing them together as a whole. Take magicians, for example. They will practise particular hand movements repetitively for hours so that they can perform them smoothly, and without having to think, when they need to do so in their shows.

remember the rest. This strategy is particularly useful when you have more than about nine bits of information to remember. So, you wouldn't necessarily need it for memorising your phone number, but you would for memorising the number of your credit card.

If you have to remember a long number, break it down into smaller chunks. Likewise, if you want to remember a piece of text, like a poem, you can also break it down into smaller chunks. If you have to remember something relatively quickly, the best way is probably to turn it into images. For example, if you had to remember a telephone number, you could break a seven-digit number down into pairs (with a single digit left over) by associating it with years, then linking them together.

Bits of information need to be 'glued' together with meaning in order to form one chunk. For example, if I gave you the following list of letters to memorise within thirty seconds, you would probably struggle:
UBSBACUCKNNMBI

But if I rearrange those letters into a list of well known acronyms, for example, with the same total letter length, you will find it easier:
USA UK IBM CNN BBC

Here, I've chunked the same number of letters into five boxes. Finally, I could take the same number of letters but in the form of just one word, and it would be incredibly easy to memorise in thirty seconds. This would

Everything should be made as simple as possible, but not simpler.
ALBERT EINSTEIN

Defining idea...

represent just one chunk. The more meaningful and less arbitrary the connections, the more likely you are to successfully chunk the information into each box.

Now, of course, it's not always possible to chunk information in such a convenient and meaningful way. You may, for example, have to remember numbers or letters which are pretty random. In which case, there are a couple of chunking strategies you can use.

Repetition: By simply breaking down the list into smaller chunks, then repeating it over and over, and adding in a rhythm to the way you are saying it, you will find the information easier to remember than in one go.

Acronyms: Your groups of letters may not naturally chunk into pre-existing acronyms like IBM, but try to group them into the first letters of words, which then form a striking story. For example, this string of letters:
PJISSMAMF
Could be turned into:
Polar bear **J**umped off **I**cecap, **S**wam **S**everal **M**iles, **A**te **M**any **F**ish.

If it's a list of numbers you need to remember, try turning the pairs of numbers into years which have some meaning to you, then link together those years into a story. For example, take this number:
63766989.

It could be split into pairs, and then I might make the following story out of them (imagining the '19' prefixing each pair): 63, I can most easily visualise this as the year that the Beatles had their first number one, so I imagine Paul McCartney. Now, 76 was the year I was born, so I might imagine Paul McCartney holding me as a baby (a frightening thought!), and 69 was the year of the first moon landing, so I imagine McCartney placing me into a moon rocket. Finally, 89 was the year the Berlin wall came down, so I imagine the moon rocket taking off but crashing into the Berlin wall.

Repetition works best if you are not under time pressure to remember your list; acronyms work best when you need to remember the list relatively quickly.

How did it go?

Q   What's the maximum amount I could remember through using chunking?

A   *In one sense, there is no maximum, as each 'bit' could trigger another bit which could trigger another, and so on. However, technically speaking, you are not holding an infinite amount of information in your working memory in that case. What you are doing is effortlessly shifting new pieces of information in and out of your working memory.*

Q   When would I want to remember a long list of letters?

A   *If you had a lot of text to memorise, you could summarise each sentence, paragraph or concept first into a word. Then take the first letter of each of these words, and your one string of letters can summarise a lot of information.*

12

How motivated are you... really?

Is the problem your memory, or are you just not interested in what you're trying to remember?

Motivation: when you've got it, almost anything is possible. But when you haven't, everything is a drag.

Trying to force yourself to learn information that are not interested in is like putting the cart before the horse. It's your motivation which provides the energy for learning. When you are highly motivated to learn about a subject, you probably will, even if your learning techniques leave much to be desired. But if you totally lack motivation, then you'll find it a struggle even if you've mastered the best learning techniques. So, before you say that you have a bad memory or that the memory techniques aren't working for you, ask yourself honestly whether you just aren't interested enough in the information you're trying to cram into your brain.

One possible reason for lack of motivation is if you are feeling depressed. There are varying degrees of depression, and all can have an effect on your memory. If you think that this could be true of you, then first look at dealing with the depression before you beat yourself up about having a bad memory. When people are

Here's an idea for you...

Crack the key to your own motivation by working out whether you are motivated more by the chance to gain pleasure or the avoidance of discomfort. Are you more motivated by risk and competition, or by safety and security? Think about how your learning goals could bring you closer to either of these two extremes. For example, learning a new language could help you have exciting foreign trips (gaining pleasure) or could mean you gain greater job security in your company.

depressed, not only do they find their memory impaired, but they are more likely to recall negative memories over positive ones. Depressed people are more likely to recall incidents in which their memories failed them, supporting their view that they have a bad memory, further undermining their memories – it becomes a self-fulfilling prophecy.

If you think you may have depression, see your doctor. However, if you think you just have a mildly depressed or negative attitude at the moment, then there are a couple of things you can do to help yourself. Firstly, exercise can be beneficial in improving mood. Try getting some regular exercise, even if it's only a brisk walk several times a week. It will also help to oxygenate your brain, improving its performance. Secondly, you should watch who you are spending time with. If you hang around with negative people, the chances are their attitudes will rub off on you. The same applies for positive people. As well as spending time with more positive-minded people, you might also like to consider finding a learning partner: someone else who is also trying to master the same knowledge. This will enable you to motivate each other. If you're trying to learn a particular subject, find someone who is enthusiastic about it. Their energy could rub off on you. If you can't find anyone, find a book by an author who is very enthused by the subject.

The ideal way to motivate yourself is to use what psychologists call 'intrinsic motivation'. This is motivation for the task itself, and not any artificial rewards that you might give yourself for completing it. For example, think about what you would enjoy learning about even if there was no extra benefit to it, such as a career boost or admiration from others. What is it about this subject that motivates you to learn more about it? The chances are you just find it fascinating. If you can find a way to find a subject fascinating, then you will have unleashed a lot of motivational energy within yourself which will help you study it.

People often say that motivation doesn't last. Well, neither does bathing – that's why we recommend it daily.
ZIG ZIGLAR, motivational speaker

Defining idea...

You could also use the power of competitiveness in order to enhance your motivation. If you have a learning partner you could engage in some friendly competition with each other to see who can learn the most, the fastest. You can also compete against yourself by striving to improve on past performance. Set yourself goals for learning, and time frames within which you would like to complete each goal. Create a basic wall chart or poster to track your progress, using something like a simple list of goals to tick off. By having this on display in your home or office, you will have a constant reminder of your progress, and a subtle daily hint to keep up your efforts in order to achieve the next learning goal.

How did it go?

Q **I have to learn something for work but I've got no natural interest in it. How can I increase my motivation?**

A *The more you learn about a subject, the more easily you can assimilate new information in it, and the more your motivation will grow. So dive in and get started, learning as much as you can, and you may find that your motivation will grow. Then, even if you feel a tiny bit more motivated, cultivate that feeling. Make a list of all the reasons why people would find that subject fascinating.*

Q **Nope, it's still not working! Any last suggestions?**

A *Create a wall chart to track your progress. This may have boxes that you colour in or tick for each section of learning you complete. Or, if all else fails, give yourself some small reward for each milestone you reach. In general this will create an inferior form of motivation to intrinsic motivation, but it will still give you some motivation.*

13

Pay attention

Information needs to go in properly if you're going to remember it, and attention has become one of the scarcest resources of our time.

Most of us don't have enough attention during the day to cover all the things we'd like it to. This lack of concentration can impair memory.

We are constantly bombarded with sensory information, yet we only consciously pay attention to a very small amount of it. In general, we only pay attention to things which are novel, emotional or meaningful. Of course, what is meaningful can vary a lot from person to person or across time, depending on the person's current range of interests. And we don't always know, at the time, what might be meaningful later. Nevertheless, somehow we must direct our attention properly if we are to learn well.

When you are trying to learn something, don't divide your attention with multitasking – performing more than one task at a time. Even if you think you are good at this, you will still be able to devote more brain power to what you're learning if you concentrate on it exclusively. Multitasking is particularly bad when you are trying to multitask using the same mode of abilities. For example, trying to

Here's an idea for you... **Ever heard the phrase 'fake it till you make it'? Often simply acting as though you were in a particular state of mind can help you get into that state. This is true of concentrated attention. Boost your attentiveness towards something by adopting the posture and facial expressions you would be using if you were naturally fascinated by it. Sit or stand upright or even lean slightly forward, and keep your eyes open wide.**

read while also listening to song lyrics will be hard, as you are using your language areas for both tasks. However, trying to read while listening to instrumental music – such as much classical music – will be easier. Pure silence is best of all. Equally, don't try and talk and read at once; both tasks require your language skills. Other distractions, such the temptation to surf the web, can be just as bad.

Getting into the optimum state of attention can be like a balancing act: too little attention and you are not processing information properly, too much alertness and you can become too anxious. This is particularly noticeable when drinking caffeinated drinks such as coffee or cola. They can be a great way to boost your attention (for a while), but too many of them, particularly on an empty stomach, can leave you feeling too anxious to concentrate well, and can also lead to tension headaches. Also, although caffeine will help increase your attention, it can also lead to an energy slump one or two hours later. For this reason, the best time to drink coffee may be an hour or two before lunch, so that you can have your energy slump in your lunch break when you don't need to concentrate so much. Or you could try drinking your caffeinated drink mid-afternoon when you will be naturally experiencing an energy slump which could affect your concentration. However, do make sure you've had a good breakfast before you drink any coffee, and you may even like to have a snack just before, or at the same time, as you drink it.

Also, in order to sustain your energy and concentration levels during the day, it's best to avoid sugary breakfasts and simple carbohydrates (like white bread). These will give an initial boost to your blood sugar, helping you concentrate, but you will soon experience a slump which makes it harder to concentrate. If you don't want this quick energy boost then slump, eat complex carbohydrates (such as vegetables and grains) instead, as these convert to sugar at a steadier pace and keep your blood sugar at a more sustained level. We all have a natural slump in blood sugar – and hence feel less energetic – around mid-afternoon. This may be an ideal time for a caffeinated drink if you need to keep your attention up till the end of the working day!

Tell me to what you pay attention and I will tell you who you are.
JOSE ORTEGA Y GASSET, philosopher

Defining idea...

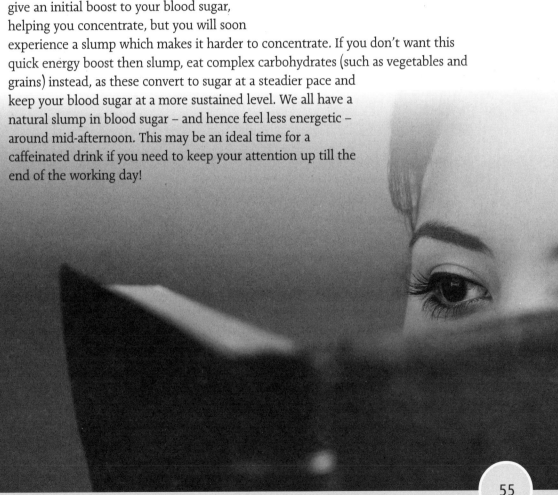

55

How did it go?

Q **How can I improve my attention when reading?**

A *Reading is one of the primary ways of learning, particularly if you are a student. Yet wading through large volumes of often dense text can tax your attention span. Before you start reading, spend a moment thinking about your goals for reading this piece of text. Think of one or several key questions that you would like to be answered by reading it. If possible, read it with a pencil in your hand. Not only will this help to guide your eye movements across the page, but you can also make (lightly, if necessary) underlinings or other markings/notes next to the most important sections. When you are then reviewing the text later, your attention can be immediately drawn to the most important bits.*

Q **How can I improve my attention when talking to people?**

If you are talking on the phone, always keep a notepad (be it digital or paper) open in front of you to capture any important pieces of information. Also, if possible, use a phone headset to free up your hands to make notes. Often, when in conversation with people, we are so keen to get our own points across that we fail to listen properly to what the other person is saying. Remind yourself to listen more carefully. Don't interrupt the person while they are in mid-flow; instead hold one hand in your pocket, with the fist lightly clenched. Each time you think of a point or question for the person, straighten one finger. This will then remind you – when it's your turn to talk – of each point or question you'd like to return.

14

The value of feedback

A little secret which will accelerate your learning speed.

Imagine a test where you were given a single final score, but didn't know which answers you'd got right. Now imagine a test in which every answer is marked...

Which do you think you'd learn more from?

Ultimately, all learning is based on the principle of feedback. The best way to learn is to make many attempts and observe the outcomes each time, modifying your behaviour accordingly. When you ignore feedback, you end up repeating the same behaviour, and your performance stagnates. Therefore, the accuracy and frequency of feedback is the mechanism that controls learning. This is also how evolution works. Nature 'tries out' many designs, and only those which survive long enough to reproduce are passed on to the next generation. Every brutal iteration improves the fitness for survival.

This type of feedback can be deliberately enhanced to improve our lives. For example, in the mid-sixteenth century two separate religious movements were founded which together came to dominate Europe: the Calvinist church in the north, the Jesuit order in the south. Writer Peter Drucker discovered what he believes to be the key to their mutual success – analysing the results of their own behaviour and feeding this

Here's an idea for you...

Trying to learn a new musical instrument? Make an audio recording of yourself just playing randomly on the instrument, then listen to it straight away. Then repeat. This creates a feedback loop that can accelerate your mastery of the instrument. The same principle was tried with babies learning to talk (their babbles were recorded and played back instantly to them), which seemed to rapidly accelerate their language development.

information back to inform future behaviour. Drucker calls this the 'feedback analysis'. 'Whenever one makes a key decision', he writes, 'and whenever one does a key action, one writes down what one expects will happen. And nine months or twelve months later one then feeds back from results to expectations. I have been doing this for some fifteen to twenty years now. And every time I do it I am surprised. And so is everyone who has ever done this.' Both the Calvinists and Jesuits used this technique, and their organisations flourished within a relatively short period of time.

FIVE RULES FOR POWERFUL FEEDBACK

1. The faster the better

Our memories learn much more easily if feedback swiftly follows actions. When one thing rapidly follows on from another, our brains can automatically assume the two are related. But the longer the gap between the two, the less likely there will be an assumed connection. For example, many people fail to make a strong connection between their reckless spending on their credit card, and the bill that then turns up at the end of the month. Seek feedback as quickly as possible after you have done something.

2. Get feedback in a real-world situation

While you can, in theory, learn to drive a car or fly a plane on a computer simulator, this is no substitute for learning in a real vehicle. Equally, you can learn a foreign language from books, DVDs and computers, but there's no real substitute for practising the language 'in the street', with real people speaking that language.

> *It is not the strongest of the species that survive, nor the most intelligent, but the ones most responsive to change.*
> CHARLES DARWIN

Defining idea...

3. Make lots of attempts

Don't think of learning as just a matter of time, but as a matter of 'cycles'. A cycle consists of one attempt, followed by feedback, followed by another attempt in the light of that feedback. The more of these cycles you can make, the faster you will learn. An example is the quick advancement of the airplane in the early twentieth century compared to that of the airship. Physicist Freeman Dyson points out that because airplanes were cheap to construct (compared to airships), they were subject to widespread experimentation (many cycles) and therefore much was learned about how to make great, safe planes in a relatively short period of time.

4. Push for improvement

After correcting your performance based on feedback, you mustn't become complacent. You must constantly strive to improve your performance. Without change, the feedback you get will just be the same each time, and you won't learn anything new. For this reason it can also be useful to simply vary your performance, and experiment with new ideas and methods.

5. Use rewards as feedback

Rewards can be a form of feedback, as they keep you 'on track' to improvement by keeping you motivated. Set goals for improvement, and give yourself a small reward on completion of each one. Alternatively, create a progress chart, with boxes to be ticked or coloured in as each stage or goal of your learning is completed. This form of reward feedback is actually more motivating than giving yourself 'treats' as rewards, as it focuses your mind on the completion of the learning as the reward in itself.

How did it go?

Q   How can I get feedback without a teacher or coach present?

A   *If you are learning something physical, you could try videoing your performance, then watch it immediately afterwards. Alternatively, keep a learning diary. Make predictions in your diary about how you expect future events to turn out based upon your current efforts, then review those predictions every few weeks, months or years. By seeing where you were correct and where you were way off, you can then improve your ability to predict outcomes.*

Q   Are there any downsides to feedback learning?

A   *Don't assume that because feedback is good, it's always good to maximise your mistakes too. We have another memory system, called implicit memory, which is extremely powerful and resilient to forgetting, but in order to use it to learn, you mustn't make mistakes. If you make mistakes, it will learn the wrong answers just as well as the right answers. So, rather than just learning by making lots of errors, take a slower approach if you can. Learn bit by bit, ensuring you have each part properly learned before testing yourself.*

15

Train your digit span

Your digit span is a little-known aspect of memory, but train it and not only will your memory improve, but you'll increase your IQ too!

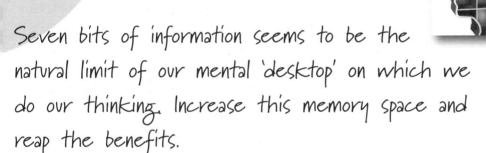

Seven bits of information seems to be the natural limit of our mental 'desktop' on which we do our thinking. Increase this memory space and reap the benefits.

Humans seem to have a predilection for the number seven; it crops up again and again through history. We talk of seven deadly sins, seas, days of the week, wonders of the world, ages of man and so on. It seems humanity never met a number seven it didn't like. Could this be related to some in-built feature of the way we think? In 1956, the psychologist George Miller published what became one of the most famous psychology papers of all time: 'The magical number seven, plus or minus two'. Miller reasoned that most people can hold in their minds between five and nine 'bits' of information. This is why telephone numbers are often seven digits long, as this is about the limit of what people can remember in one go.

This limited amount of information is referred to as our digit span, or working memory. Working memory is like the desktop of the mind: it's where our brains do their conscious thinking work. Information is constantly flowing into and out of our

Here's an idea for you...

Keep an eye out for games that will help you to practise holding lots of information in your mind at once. There are many card and video games which require players to memorise a number of bits of information. These will enable you to increase the volume of information you can hold at once in your working memory, while also having fun.

working memory. It is also referred to as short-term memory, as it rarely lasts more than about thirty seconds. In order to make judgements and calculations we need to use our working memory. When asked to distinguish between musical tones, for example, people can distinguish between no more than about six. This is nothing to do with our hearing abilities; it seems that we can typically only distinguish between about seven categories of items at once due to our working memory. Equally, if you quickly flash up a number of dots on a computer screen and ask people to tell you how many there were, once you use more than around seven dots, people start to make errors. Fewer than seven dots and they accurately count them; more than seven and they will guess.

So, is this an in-built limit of our brains? It seems it might be. The explanation is technical, but it seems that it's to do with the interplay of two frequency patterns in our cortex (the uppermost part of the brain, which is more developed in humans than animals). One frequency, called theta, is the neurons firing at around five times per second, another, called gamma, fires at around thirty-five times per second. One theory is that the number of gamma pulses you have for every theta pulse is what determines your digit span. In other words, thirty-five divided by five is seven. The theory seems to make sense, but no one really knows at the moment if it's actually true.

The implication of this is that it's best to organise information – both for yourself and others – into no more than seven categories. Think of them as seven boxes which you can use to put information in. If you can pack the information tightly together, then you can get more than one thing in each box. For example, if you have two or three bits of information that are closely linked in your mind, so that the mere mention of one of them will trigger the other bits, then that one group will only use up one of your seven boxes. Therefore you can increase the amount you can hold in your working memory by making close associations between individual bits of information.

The span of absolute judgment and the span of immediate memory impose severe limitations on the amount of information that we are able to receive, process and remember.
GEORGE A. MILLER, psychologist

Defining idea...

Working memory varies between individuals, and seems to account for between about a quarter and a half of the variation in intelligence between individuals. In other words, the greater your working-memory capacity, the greater your intelligence is likely to be. There's also evidence suggesting that by training yourself you can increase your digit span, and therefore increase your intelligence and ability to concentrate on information. To train your digit span, write out several series of numbers, gradually increasing their length. Read each series out once, then look away and try to recall it in reverse order. Start with around seven numbers, and make sure you can easily handle that, before moving onto eight and so on.

How did it go?

Q **Are there any other ways to improve my working memory in everyday life?**

A *Yes, cut out distractions. If you need to concentrate when you are working, seek out a quiet environment. You can also try making notes and talking to yourself to increase your ability to hold lots of information in mind. Writing things down releases a bit of the pressure of holding information in the mind all at once.*

Q **How can I keep information in my working memory?**

A *It seems that maintaining information in working memory mainly works in terms of sound, rather than images or concepts. In other words, you imagine the sound – such as the sound of yourself speaking the information – over and over in order to hold onto it. You've probably experienced this when trying to remember a phone number you've just heard while searching for something on which to write it down!*

16

Memory supplements

Pop a pill and instantly boost your memory? It's an attractive idea, but can it work?

Wouldn't it be great if boosting your memory was as simple as buying a bottle of pills?

There are a lot of supplements available which claim to improve memory. These range from smart drugs (so-called 'nootropics'), to amino acids, to hormones and vitamins. Some of these have been around for a long time. For example, the herb rosemary has long been claimed to improve memory, although there is not yet any scientific evidence for this. Recent years have seen an explosion of memory enhancing supplements. The most famous is probably *Ginkgo biloba*. However, the evidence for such supplements, including ginkgo, actually creating any significant boost in memory abilities is inconclusive at best, non-existent at worst.

I won't exhaustively list all the supplements which have failed to show any evidence for memory improvements, but I will mention a few that have shown *some* evidence...

There is fairly good evidence that beta-carotene can help protect against dementias, but only if taken over the long term. A study of over 4000 men taking a beta-carotene supplement since 1982 showed that they scored significantly better on

Be aware of the placebo effect: the tendency for some medical supplements to 'work' simply because we expect them to. Some studies have found that the power of belief can be so strong that the benefits are actually real, and not just imagined. However, don't be convinced to buy expensive memory-boosting products just on the basis of a recommendation from a friend. The only things which can provide solid evidence for whether such products work are good scientific studies.

memory tests than those who took a placebo. However, those who had only been taking it for a year showed no difference.

Another supplement which has evidence for memory-boosting properties is folic acid. Older men and women in the Netherlands took part in a study taking this supplement and subsequent memory tests showed that their memories were the equivalent of people five years younger than they actually were. However, many foods, such as green vegetables, already contain folic acid. Also, there is a risk with taking increased amounts of folic acid; it can mask a vitamin B12 deficiency in the elderly. Currently, the only people most doctors advise to take increased amounts of folic acid are pregnant women.

Finally, chromium picolinate was given to twenty-one older adults with signs of memory decline; then they had functional magnetic resonance imaging (fMRI) brain scans. The scans, claimed the researchers, showed increased activity in an area of the brain associated with memory. They concluded that older adults may benefit from taking this supplement. However, the sample size was relatively small and funding for the study was provided by the company who sell the supplement (although the study was conducted scientifically).

It's possible that memory supplements may have a small benefit which studies so far have not been able to demonstrate conclusively and repeatedly. It's also possible that they may have a beneficial effect on some people but not in general meaning that, overall, studies would not show any effect. Finally, it is also perfectly possible that new drugs will be developed in the future that will significantly boost memory. But we are not there yet.

Everything is being compressed into tiny tablets.
WALTER CRONKITE, American journalist

Defining idea...

In the meantime, if you are looking for a physical way to improve your memory, a balanced, healthy diet and regular exercise are your best options. One addition you may like to make to your diet is more food or drinks which contain antioxidants, such as fruit, vegetables and green tea. Oxidation is thought to be involved in dementias such as Alzheimer's. Research done with older dogs showed that when fed antioxidant-rich foods over the course of several years, their memories improved significantly. Foods rich in antioxidants which may be particularly beneficial include berries (blueberries, blackberries, strawberries, etc.), plums, oranges, grapes, spinach, broccoli and onions.

The concept of memory pills is a seductive one, as it appears to offer a simple and effortless route to memory enhancement. People are very receptive to it, and many have been given more confidence in these products by their fancy-sounding names than they, perhaps, should have. However, most memory improvements are active, rather than passive processes. In order to get the most benefits, you need to put some work in.

How did it go?

Q   So would you recommend I take any supplements to boost my memory?

A   *The short answer is no. There are more powerful ways to boost your memory, even in old age, such as exercise and good diet. However, if your doctor advises you to take a particular dietary supplement (for example, because of a mineral deficiency), and lack of this supplement may affect your brain functioning, then doing so will help prevent memory problems. But currently the evidence is not strong enough to compel me to recommend these supplements for general use. Equally, if you are prescribed a specific drug to treat dementia, then by all means take it, as these are a different type of drug from those I'm talking about here.*

Q   If I read of a study which shows a particular supplement works, how do I know whether to believe it?

A   *Ask yourself a few basic questions about the study, like these. Who funded it? (If the drug company that seeks to market the supplement funded the study, then you may have reason to question it.) How large was the sample size? (A few tens of people is far less significant than hundreds.) Who or what was the study done on? (If the study was performed, for example, on rats, then it might not have the same effect on humans. If the study was performed on a particular population of humans, such as older females, it might not necessarily have the same effect on everyone else.)*

17

Creative concept mapping

Getting more creative with taking notes can boost your memory.

Each memory stored within your cortex is connected to many associated memories, like a network. Concept maps mimic the way your memory works, making it easier to learn and recall information.

Taking notes the traditional way, while being very useful, has its drawbacks. The main one is that it's usually linear. So, it's great for making lists or sequences of information, but not so good at 'nested' structures of knowledge. What do I mean by nested? Basically any information which has layers in which there are some elements which can be broken down into sub-elements, a little like a large company can be broken down into its departments, which then each have head managers and workers under those managers. It's quite an organic, tree-like structure. If you drew a diagram of a typical company's structure, this would be a concept map. Such inter-relationships are important for remembering information, but typically get lost when you make notes in the ordinary way. Concept maps show the structure or organisation of a body of knowledge, or how its pieces connect together.

Here's an idea for you...

Even if you don't use mind-mapping, you can make your regular notes more memorable simply by adding different colours and sketches to your text. This will involve more parts of your brain, giving it a greater chance to memorise the information. Developing your drawing abilities will also help strengthen your visualisation skills, which are at the core of many memory strategies.

Mind maps™, or 'spidergrams' are a form of concept mapping and are an incredibly versatile and powerful technique. They are less diagrammatic, and instead use what's called a radial hierarchy. This means that you begin with the main theme in the middle of the page, then the key concepts emanate from that theme, and then sub-concepts branch off from each of those.

They can be used in all sorts of situations, from brainstorming creative ideas to taking notes on a lecture, revising for an exam and planning anything from a holiday to a new business. The

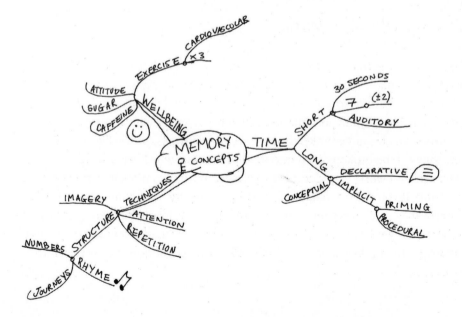

(Mind Maps are a trademark of the Buzan Organization Ltd)

method is so versatile that it's been called the 'Swiss army knife' of thinking techniques. The author and psychologist Tony Buzan has developed it, and emphasises several rules which will help you make your own: use colour, use only one word per line, and be as creative/versatile as you like (use drawings, numbered lists, diagrams). On the opposite page is an example of one of mine

A mind map is a thinking tool which reflects, externally, what goes on inside your head.
TONY BUZAN, author, psychologist and developer of the mind-mapping technique

Defining idea...

In terms of learning and memorising, Mind Maps have several important advantages over making ordinary notes. Firstly, they engage more parts of your brain, meaning you are more likely to remember them. By using the space of the paper more creatively and encouraging you to use colour and graphics, they engage your visual skills more. You are more likely to remember information if it has a spatial position, and these give each piece of information their own meaningful position on a page. Secondly, simply by creating the map, you are forced to think about the information, and find its structure. This encourages you to understand the information and process it more deeply, meaning you are more likely to remember it. Lastly, Mind Maps reduce the burden on your short-term memory by allowing you to get all the information you need on a subject 'out of your head' and onto paper, in a meaningful and organised way. This allows you to then get an overview of what you know, and will tend to prompt other ideas in a way I've found much more powerful than traditional notes. They make it far easier to recall information. If you are trying to replicate a set of linear notes, it can be very tricky. That's because our short-term memory is limited – we can only hold so much sequenced information in the mind at once.

Think of it this way: if you had to draw a sketch, is it easier to start with the rough outline and fill in the details, or to begin at the top corner and move slowly to the right, putting in every detail, with little opportunity to go back to put in the bits you forget?

How did it go?

Q I'm just not good at drawing, even a straight line eludes me! Is this technique for me?

A *Definitely: this is not an art competition! You don't have to be a Picasso to use this technique. Your maps can be as messy as you like, and they certainly don't rely on straight lines: have your lines as wonky as you like, too.*

Q Isn't there software for constructing these kind of maps?

A *Yes, there are a number of software packages. However, having played around with a few of them, my feeling is that good old-fashioned paper is still best for these. Until everyone has really good touch-screens which would allow you to write onto the computer freehand, rather than use a mouse and keyboard, the computer somehow gets in the way of the process and makes it feel more awkward and less 'free flowing' than doing it on paper.*

18

Sleep on it

Your sleeping brain makes memories stronger.

Do you ever feel deprived of sleep?
With busy modern lifestyles, many of us
are getting less sleep than we used to.
This could be harmful to your memory.

We spend up to a third of our lives asleep, yet scientists still don't quite understand why. However, new research suggests that sleep and dreaming are important for organising and storing long-term memories. For example, while scientists still don't fully understand the purpose of dreaming, many believe it is at least partially responsible for helping us consolidate our memories into long-term storage. Is it any coincidence that the incongruous and emotional imagery that memory experts recommend to use in forming mental journeys and stories is so similar to dreaming? Also, if you've ever spent a few hours playing video games in the evening, you may have had the experience of 'seeing' the game still playing when you close your eyes to sleep that night. Evidence from both rats and humans suggests that spatial routes learned during the day are mentally rehearsed during sleep: the same sequences of brain activity that occurred during the daytime learning were seen in their sleeping brains. What we've learned during the day could be sorted and stored during dreaming at night.

Here's an idea for you...

Try the following to get a good night's sleep: avoid caffeinated drinks for at least four hours before bedtime, try to get some exercise during the day and as much natural light during the day as you can. If possible, don't work or watch TV in your bedroom. Dim the lights a short time before bed, and do something relaxing, such as taking a hot bath or drinking a hot (non-caffeinated!) drink. Avoid watching exciting TV shows or concentrating on anything demanding of your attention for an hour before bedtime.

In people who've undergone severe sleep deprivation (i.e. days without sleep), hallucinations are a common side effect. It's almost as though the brain has to dream regularly in order to stay sane. It's also the case that even mild sleep deprivation will impair your memory: you'll probably find yourself forgetting even basic things when you are very tired. But, crucially, you won't feel like your memory is suffering: sleep-deprived people are completely confident that they are correct about their recollections. And don't assume coffee will cure this: it will give a temporary boost, but doesn't cure the memory problems.

Equally, younger people seem to need more sleep than older people, and the former (particularly babies, who sleep for about twelve hours a day) have more information to lay down into memories. Of course, it could be that younger people need more sleep because their bodies are growing. Yet, the process of memories strengthening is itself a little like physical growth, but on a tiny scale: the strengthening of connections between neurons in the brain. This is a crucial part of forming memories, and it appears to occur during sleep. However, there is only strong evidence that this improves learning for physical movements, for example, if you were learning to touch-type or to play tennis, and not for learning facts. In fact, even a long nap (an hour and a half) can improve learning for physical skills. This isn't to say that if you are a student, for example, revising for exams, that sleep isn't important; merely that scientists have not found strong evidence that it is. However, sleep may have secondary benefits to developing a good memory for facts, such as increasing your ability to concentrate during the day. So, if you are trying to learn new information, get a good night's sleep the night before studying, as well as afterwards.

Sleep is when all the unsorted stuff comes flying out as from a dustbin upset in a high wind.
WILLIAM G. GOLDING, novelist and poet

Defining idea...

Nevertheless, sleep does seem to help us remember things we had forgotten during the day. It's almost as though, during sleep, our brain searches through the thoughts and memories of the day, like a nocturnal secretary, and places the important ones into our mental in-tray for the following morning. Also, many people find that if they go to sleep thinking about a problem, they can often wake up with a solution.

Are you getting enough sleep? How much is enough? Experts recommend about seven to eight hours, although it can vary from person to person, and there has even been some research showing that women may, on average, need an hour's more sleep than men. The key thing is to stick to a regular sleeping pattern so that your body can maintain a regular rhythm. Try to get up at the same time every day, even on weekends. If you don't get enough sleep, or sleep poorly, resist the temptation to lie in bed in the morning, and instead, if possible, have a fifteen-minute nap, mid-afternoon.

How did it go?

Q **Can you learn during your sleep by listening to audio tracks?**

A *Unfortunately the research doesn't back up this claim. During sleep you are focused inwards, not outwards. However, you could listen to information on audio tracks before going to sleep, as this might help you encode the information.*

Q **I've heard that any sleep you get before midnight is worth more than after midnight. Is this true?**

A *Not exactly. There's nothing special about midnight, but what is true is that the earlier in the evening you go to sleep, the more deep, dreamless sleep you will experience, and the more you sleep on in the morning, the more dreaming sleep. But as we don't yet fully understand the contributions made by dreaming and non-dreaming sleep to learning, it's difficult to say which is better for your memory. One current theory is that dreaming sleep helps memories for physical movements and spatial locations, while deeper sleep helps memories for facts.*

19

Smells familiar?

Smell is the most primal and fundamental of our senses and is a powerful trigger for memories. All our senses can provoke memories, but none are better than smell.

We don't know why smells are such a powerful trigger of memories. However, there are some clues as to why this should be.

Firstly, our sense of smell is very closely linked to our emotions, and emotions are a powerful trigger for memory. Most of the time, the memories that smells evoke have a strong emotional tone to them. Indeed, the olfactory nerve is very closely connected to the amygdala, an area of the brain which deals with primal emotions, particularly fear. It's likely that our emotions actually evolved out of our sense of smell, as it would have been useful, even for a simple organism, to tell from the chemicals in the environment whether it should move away from a predator or towards food. Also, the olfactory nerve is closely connected to the hippocampi, the areas of the brain responsible for recording most of our long-term memories.

Much of our sense of smell seems to be subconscious, and some of it is hard wired by evolution. Surprisingly, we can learn to recognise people by their unique scent (everyone has one). We are probably doing this all the time, although it happens

Here's an idea for you...

Strengthen your conscious awareness of scents. Take a moment to smell the air wherever you are now. Is the odour pleasant, neutral or unpleasant? Do this each time you enter a new environment.

subliminally, below our level of conscious awareness. We're also continually testing the quality of the air around us, as we are able to detect odours at a distance. This is an unconscious habit that probably evolved in order to protect us from danger; the ability, for example, to smell traces of smoke in the air could be a useful early warning for danger. We also have an in-built ability to identify bad smells; even a one-day-old baby recoils and makes a face at the smell of rotten eggs or fish.

Because our smell-memory system is largely subconscious, it means that it's both more powerful yet more inaccessible than other forms of memory. As mentioned, it has a powerful ability to trigger memories. Just one sniff of the right smell can take us back to a time in childhood, maybe even one we'd long forgotten.

Smell can enhance the ability to learn. You may like to experiment with learning something in the presence of a particular scent, then use that scent again when trying to recall the information. In a recent study, people who revised information while in the presence of a rose scent, and then had the scent around them while they slept that night, scored 15% higher on a test of the information they'd revised. However, while you could use this technique, it is a little bit tricky. The scent must be inhaled during the deeper, slow-wave periods of sleep, rather than the lighter, rapid-eye-movement stages of sleep, which are closely associated with dreaming. You can't just inhale the scent all night, as your brain can become accustomed to it over time and it loses its potency (just as, after some time, the sound of a ticking clock fades into the background).

This is easily achieved in a sleep laboratory, but I expect that you don't have a team of scientists in lab coats in your bedroom while you sleep, who could helpfully hold the correct scent under your nostrils at the right moment. However, if you were motivated and ingenious enough, you could achieve this. One fact about sleep that will help you, is that you experience most of your deeper sleep at the beginning of the night. So, for example, you could put the scent in front of a fan, facing your bed, then place the fan on a timer, so that it was only on during the first hour or two of sleep. Alternatively, you could use a plug-in room fragrance product that gives off a scent only for a limited time. The technique may also work simply by having the scent near you, and taking an extended (about an hour) nap, although no research has been done to test this yet.

Odour memory seems to be the most resistant to forgetting.

DR JAY GOTTFRIED, scent researcher

Defining idea...

How did it go?

Q Given how difficult the scent-while-sleeping technique is, would you recommend it?

A *I'd say it's a more advanced memory technique for those seeking an edge in their ability to learn new information. Don't use it as your only memory technique, but feel free to experiment with adding it to your repertoire once you've already mastered other memory-boosting methods.*

Q I'm learning to drive. Could I use the scent-while-sleeping technique to inhale the same scent as the car's air freshener?

A *No. The scent-while-sleeping technique only works for learning factual information, rather than physical movement information (such as learning to drive, type or ski). However, you might like, if possible, to use the same car air freshener in the car you learn in and the one you will be tested in. You could have the same air freshener around when revising the theoretical driving information as you do when you are tested on that, too.*

Q If smells are so powerful in provoking recall, is there any way I can harness this?

A *Often a smell will trigger a powerful feeling of familiarity, but you won't necessarily be able to consciously describe what the smell actually is. If you learn to identify smells – simply by paying more attention to them, and always making an effort to identify them – you can increase your ability to put a name to familiar scents. Then, rather than just think 'Hm, that's really familiar' or 'Oh, that reminds me of my school days or my grandparents' house', you'll know exactly the source of the scent.*

20

Think positive

Positive thinking has become a cliché of the self-improvement movement. But it bears mentioning that it really can help boost your memory.

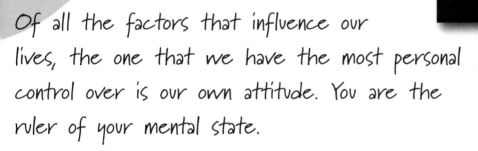

Of all the factors that influence our lives, the one that we have the most personal control over is our own attitude. You are the ruler of your mental state.

Our memories are not like those of a computer chip; our brain functions are heavily influenced by our emotional state. Information, for example, learned while we are emotionally aroused is more likely to be remembered, and particularly so if we are positively aroused. However, if you try to learn something and then experience a strong emotion straight afterwards, that event can block your ability to store the memory of the thing you were trying to learn.

Positive mood can improve our ability to recall both emotionally neutral and positive information. Its effects on our memory abilities probably have something to do with the fact that dopamine (a brain chemical) levels rise in the frontal lobes (the region of the brain which co-ordinates our retrieval of information from memory) when we feel good. In other words, a positive mood changes the neuro-chemistry of the brain in such a way that you're better able to remember.

Here's an idea for you...

A quick method of improving your mood is simply to act as though you were already feeling positive. Try straightening up your posture, so that you look confident and energetic. Next, put a broad smile on your face (OK, you may feel a bit silly doing this if you are in a public place, although you may also make some new friends!). Just the act of using your facial smile muscles gets you into a happy frame of mind. Even if it doesn't make you feel instantly blissful, keep it up for a few minutes. At the worst you'll find it hard to be negative.

Being depressed may affect your memory, although not necessarily always directly. Some studies have shown that those who are mildly depressed do not have an impaired ability to recall information. Other studies show that depression creates a bias in the types of emotional information recalled: if you feel bad, you are more likely to recall negative memories. However, being depressed will almost certainly weaken your ability to learn and memorise information. You will most likely suffer from lower levels of motivation and concentration: you just can't keep your mind on the task, and can't be bothered to learn. Therefore, if you think you may be depressed – even mildly – it might be worth consulting your doctor to deal with that problem before assuming you just have a bad memory.

If you hold negative beliefs about your own memory abilities, then you could be creating a self-fulfilling prophecy that subsequently lowers your ability to remember! It may, for example, even be the case that much of the decline in memory associated with old age is due to negative stereotypes about ageing. Everyone is familiar with the idea that their memory declines with age. People are mostly resigned to it. Birthday cards joke about it. People use it as an excuse when they can't remember something. In experiments, people primed with negative words – such as senile and incompetent – subsequently performed worse on memory tests than those primed with words like alert and wise. Therefore, even when we are not consciously aware of them (or maybe especially when!), our memory performance is affected by negative concepts. Remember that memory decline with age isn't inevitable: there can be an increase in memory skills with age, as those who are older have a larger 'databank' of memories on which to draw. Emulate the Chinese, who have a more positive attitude towards ageing, and emphasise the wisdom that comes from an old memory, rather than any potential decline.

If people can suppress negative thoughts, they will do much better, and a positive attitude can promote effective functioning.
PROFESSOR THOMAS HESS, on a study showing that negative stereotypes affect memory performance in older adults

Defining idea...

In our memories, we tend to exaggerate how bad something felt, and hence dread it more in the future. Keep a diary, and at the end of days or weeks in which something bad has happened, write about it. You will soon learn that you are more emotionally resilient to negative events than you thought, and most worries merely spring from the tendency to overexaggerate such negative memories.

The link between positive emotions and memory can also run in the opposite direction: we can use our memories to help us feel more positive. Try making a list of ten occasions in the past when you've felt very happy. Squeeze as much detail out of each of these memories as you can. Try to recall information from all your senses: what sounds, textures, scents, temperatures, etc., were present? Then, whenever you are feeling down, replay one of these memories, and imagine you are re-experiencing all those sensory details.

How did it go?

Q   Are there any downsides to positive emotion from the point of view of memory?

A   *If you allow yourself to become complacent, then, yes, you could impair your memory abilities. Also, if you are feeling so ebullient or excited that you are distracted, then you may not be able to learn information as well.*

Q   And are there any other ways I can improve how I feel in everyday life?

A   *People definitely differ in their general levels of happiness, and this seems to be more due to genetics than to their situation in life. However, there are a few things you can do to improve your general mood: get regular exercise, don't compare yourself too much with others and don't always take failures personally.*

21

State-dependent memory

Emotions and memory are closely linked. Your emotional state of mind at the time you learn information can affect how easily you recall that information later.

When we learn something, we are also storing information about the time, place and our emotional state. These can then act as cues or triggers that help us remember.

Emotions can heighten our memories. As an extreme example, soldiers who experience an horrific incident during war often can recall it in great detail and, whenever they experience similar things, can have vivid 'flashbacks' of the incident. Two things are happening here. Firstly, our brains are naturally biased towards remembering highly emotional events (as these are typically more significant to us, and potentially important to our future survival). Secondly, things that we associated with a memory at the time it was formed can themselves act as powerful triggers for replaying that memory.

Memory triggers can be external (things happening around you, or the environment you are in) or internal (your emotional state). One experiment showed the effect our external environment can have by getting people to try to learn words while under water and back on dry land. Those words learned underwater

Ask yourself what kind of situation you will be in when you will need to recall the information you're trying to remember. Will it be in a quiet room (as in an exam) or in a busy city centre (as when you are using a foreign language), or even under water (when learning scuba diving)? Practise as much as you can within that environment, as learning which takes place there will be easier to recall there.

were more easily recalled under water, and the same for those on land. However, this effect only seems to hold for major changes to the environment; simply moving from one room into another will not have much, if any, effect on your ability to recall information. Other experiments have shown that when people learn information while drunk, they are better at recalling that same information when they are drunk again than when they are sober. There have even been reports of people hiding money or alcohol when drunk, being unable to find it when they sober up, but then able to recall its hiding place when drunk again. Similar effects have been found for people learning information when consuming caffeine or smoking cigarettes.

Interestingly, for both these internal and external triggers, it's recall that is affected, not recognition. The former is when you're asked to supply the information learned, the latter is when you're asked to select the answer from a given range of options.

There are two different types of state-dependent memory. The first is when you are more likely to remember information when you are in the same state of mind as when you learned it (as in the example of the drunks). The second is when you are more likely to remember a certain type of information depending on your state of mind. For example, when you are in a happy mood you're more likely to remember happy memories, and the opposite when you are feeling down. The stronger the emotion, the greater the effect. It also seems to be the case that negative moods have a more powerful memory effect than positive ones.

Anything experienced in a given mood state will tend to be recalled more easily when that mood is reinstated.
ALAN BADDELEY, memory expert

Defining idea...

Sometimes, the way in which we learn information can be so important that it becomes harder to recall that information in a different context. For example, if you are taught something verbally, it will probably be easier for you to recall it in a verbal fashion than in a visual fashion, and vice versa. If you learn information on a computer, but then are tested on paper, your ability to recall the information may not be as great as if you were tested on a computer, and vice versa. This could be related to what psychologists call 'muscle memory', which is the way that physical skills requiring complex movements that are hard to learn can be triggered again quickly, once learned, if we have the right 'prop' in front of us. For example, you may not have ridden a bicycle or played tennis for years, but once you get back on the saddle, or get the racket in your hand, the muscle memory for how to move comes flooding back quickly.

So, what are the implications of this? Essentially, you can boost your ability to recall if you give yourself the internal and external cues that you were experiencing when you originally learned the information. For example, if you are struggling to remember something, think back to the time you learned it. Where were you? Could you visit that place? Just walking around it will trigger many memories. What foods and drinks were you in the habit of consuming at the time? Try them again (especially if you haven't for a while), and see what memories they evoke.

How did it go?

Q I find it hard to stay positive as I tend to ruminate over negative memories a lot, which then only makes me more likely to remember other negative memories! What can I do about this?

A *Make an effort to improve your mood and recall happy memories. Put up photos of happy occasions in your working environment so you will see them during the day.*

Q Do any other emotional states have an effect on my ability to memorise information?

A *If you are anxious or worried, this can impair your ability to learn information. It may be because your worries are eating away at your attention, and therefore you have less to give to whatever it is you might be learning. Be sure to pay attention to your emotions when learning anything important. If you find yourself becoming anxious while attempting to learn something, first try to calm yourself down.*

22

Tip of the tongue

'Oh, I know the word! It's... um... I definitely know it! It's right on the tip of my tongue!'

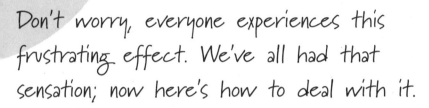

Don't worry, everyone experiences this frustrating effect. We've all had that sensation; now here's how to deal with it.

Pioneering nineteenth-century psychologist, William James, described this as a 'gap that is intensely active'. You have a strong conviction you should know the word. Yet despite trying hard, you just can't recall it. Most of us know it as the 'tip of the tongue' effect. It typically happens when you're trying to remember someone's name or a particular word (rather than, for example, a date or spatial location). It's a linguistic problem: we can't find the word, even though we can easily 'picture the face', or know the meaning, or know roughly how the word should sound.

Research has shown that young people experience this, on average, between once and twice a week, while the number doubles for older people. However often it happens, the experience of tip of the tongue is usually very frustrating and consumes your attention until you have recalled the hidden bit of information.

Interestingly, in virtually all languages which have a term for this effect, it refers to the tongue as though there was something specifically going on about the speech mechanism. This seems to have some truth in it. For example, when people can't

Here's an idea for you...

If you can't remember a name, try running through the alphabet, starting by asking yourself 'Does it begin with "a"?' and so on. This method might seem long winded, but you should be able to move through the alphabet within a few minutes, and it typically takes more than a few minutes to otherwise remember a name which is on the tip of your tongue. Once you've found the letter that it begins with, this is often enough to trigger the memory of the word.

remember a name they can often picture the face of the person, showing that it's the verbal and not the visual information that is the source of the problem.

An experiment conducted with people suspected of Alzheimer's disease showed that when they experienced the tip of the tongue effect, their guesses were more often related to the meaning of the word, whereas other adults guessing are just as likely to provide guesses which *sound* like the word. Interestingly, some research shows that emotional words take longer to recall than non-emotional words. Usually people can describe things about the word, such as words it sounds like, or how many syllables it has.

There are two reasons why people experience this effect.

Firstly, we can usually think of another word which we think is similar. However, this can often be the biggest problem: the similar word can block the emergence of the actual one. No matter how much you try, you just can't get that wrong word out of your mind. The only way to deal with this is to relax and try to consciously let go of trying to remember. These blocking words cannot be removed by force!

The other time we experience it is when we don't actually know the word in the first place, but we know enough about the subject to think we *might* know the answer. Also, what sometimes happens is that when we are asked a question which is a little bit too difficult for us to answer, our brains often supply the answer to a simpler, related question. This can create a situation similar to the first type of tip of the tongue, where a wrong word is blocking the correct one. Only in this instance we have a wrong answer, but it's not blocking the right answer because we don't know the right answer. An example of this is when people are asked to name the capital of Australia. Sydney comes to mind, even though this is incorrect. The correct answer, Canberra, is not so easily visualised or brought to mind as it is less well known. Often, people don't so much genuinely think that Sydney is the capital, they just find it pops into their mind more quickly.

Your memory is a monster; you forget – it doesn't. It simply files things away. It keeps things for you, or hides things from you – and summons them to your recall with a will of its own. You think you have a memory; but it has you!
JOHN IRVING

Defining idea...

So, what should you do when you experience tip of the tongue? First of all, decide whether you definitely know the word, or whether you just think you might. If you don't know the word to begin with, then it's obviously not a memory problem! If you do know it, try to think of as many things about it as you can. Things about the meaning of it, as well as things about the way it sounds. Finally, if you still can't remember it, or if you have a word which is constantly blocking you from remembering it, then just stop trying to remember. Put it aside, and the chances are it will pop into your memory of its own accord soon enough.

How did it go?

Q **I experience tip of the tongue a lot. Does this mean I'm losing my memory or that I have a bad memory?**

A *Maybe, but not necessarily. Virtually everyone experiences this. If you experience it more often than you think other people do, then it could just be that you're distracted a lot and thinking of other things.*

Q **Are there ways to avoid tip of the tongue?**

A *Not really, as it tends to occur for random things, such as obscure words or the names of actors from old films. In other words, things which you couldn't necessarily predict you would need to know. If you are regularly experiencing this with the names of people you should know, then try to make a meaningful connection between something about that person (such as their job or a prominent physical feature) and their name. If you are experiencing it for technical terms that you need for work, then you can put some extra effort into learning those words.*

23

Priming

When we see or hear about something, all sorts of memories are triggered in our subconscious mind.

These then have a sneaky influence on how we think and act next. Some memories influence us without our conscious awareness.

Have you ever felt sad for no particular reason, then traced the feeling back to something you saw or heard earlier in the day which reminded you of a sad episode in the past? Your unconscious brain can be like a well-prepared personal assistant who pulls out files relating to current projects just in case you might need them. The reason for this is that the brain is trying to predict the kind of responses you might have to make in the near future, and prepare you for them. Psychologists call this effect 'priming'.

There are two types of priming. Perceptual priming is when your senses are primed by something. This could be the way something looks, sounds or feels. Conceptual priming is when things within the same category or of similar meaning are primed. For example, seeing the word 'table' will probably prime the concepts relating to furniture (conceptual priming); hearing the word 'table' may prime the word 'stable', which sounds similar, but has a totally unrelated meaning (perceptual priming).

Here's an idea for you...

Be aware of the effect of the language you use when talking to people. Different words can subconsciously prime different memories in people, and cause them to react in different ways without realising it. If you want to motivate a person, for example, try using language which they will associate with energising and positive memories.

Priming may trigger particular goals or intentions we already have, but which are not currently active. As an example, in one experiment, participants who were filling in a questionnaire were given a crumbly snack which made a slight mess on the floor. Half of the participants were in a room containing a citrus scent, reminiscent of cleaning products. Those participants were significantly more likely to clean up their crumbs than those who were in a room with no scent. People may have a vague intention to always clean up after themselves, but it took the citrus scent to prime that intention into action.

Priming can also affect how we perceive or categorise things. For example, one experiment had a lab assistant ask people to hold a cup. Later, they were asked to rate the assistant's personality. Those people who'd been asked to hold a cup of hot coffee rated the assistant as being 'warmer' than those who'd been asked to hold a cup containing a cold drink, who attributed more 'cold' qualities to the assistant's personality!

If priming is so powerful, and operates unconsciously, what can we do about it? Be as aware as you can of the effect that your surroundings have on your ability to recall information. For example, if you are in depressing surroundings, then you are more likely to bring to mind depressing memories and, conversely, happy surroundings enable us to more easily recall positive memories. This not only applies to your physical environment, but to the people around you. However, this also means that it's hard to consciously use priming on yourself – if you are aware of it, it won't work. The only way you might be able to do this is to place priming items in your environment then leave them there long enough to forget why you put them there. Such items might include props, posters or postcards to remind you of any ongoing goals, such as to be more productive, positive or frugal. Also, if you are having trouble remembering something, you can prime your memory by just thinking of similar things, or things that are likely to be connected. If you do this, then the thing you have forgotten may itself be activated. Although most of us do this naturally anyway.

We have unconscious behavioural guidance systems that are continually furnishing suggestions through the day about what to do next, and the brain is acting on those, all before conscious awareness.
JOHN A. BARGH, psychologist

Defining idea...

How did it go?

Q I've heard about subliminal messages in advertisements priming people to do things. Should I be worried about this?

A *There's no clear-cut answer to this. Although the effects of subliminal messages are not as powerful as you may think, they sometimes may work. A belief in subliminal messages in advertising mainly stems from a 1950s, study which claimed cinema-goers were more likely to buy snacks if they'd been exposed to one single frame (i.e. below their level of conscious awareness) showing a bag of popcorn and a cola drink. However, the study was later found to be a fake. The key thing is, though, that it's merely triggering something (a concept or goal) within our brain that is already there. There's no evidence that you can be primed to do something that is against your will or your value system. However, the way you categorise information could certainly be influenced by the words with which you are primed. Also, priming could trigger stereotyped behaviour.*

Q Can I use knowledge of priming to improve my thinking in general?

A *When we make decisions, we sometimes draw upon our gut feelings. Memory priming influences the gut feelings you have, which are often highly accurate without us knowing why. As we can unconsciously process a greater array of information than we can do consciously (with our limited attention or digit spans) we're able to access more of our memory databanks with gut feelings than with conscious thought. The rule of thumb is that if the decision is simple, work out the best option consciously; if it's complex, go with your gut feeling.*

24
Using the 80/20 rule

Ever noticed that often small things can make big differences? It can happen across all fields of life, including memory. Scientists refer to it as the 80/20 principle.

In most areas of life, 80% of the results flow from 20% of the causes. Here's how to focus your energy on this most effective 20%.

The 80/20 principle was first noticed by a nineteenth-century Italian economist called Vilfredo Pareto. He observed that in his country a minority of people owned the majority of wealth, and a minority of people earned the majority of incomes. Not necessarily an amazing observation, you might think. However, the interesting thing was that Pareto discovered almost precisely the same distribution in any country he looked at, and from any period in the past. Since then the rule – in its broadest sense of a minority of factors resulting in the majority of causes – has been observed all over the place, from politics to economics, and to people's personal lives.

In business, for example, roughly 20% of a company's or shop's products account for 80% of sales. In everyday life, probably around 20% of your clothes get about 80% of the wear. Wherever you look, you can find examples of the principle. However, an important thing to note is that the ratio isn't always exactly 80:20, nor

Use the 80/20 law when learning a new language or when learning specialist terms within a particular subject. Even though any language has a huge vocabulary, and many specialisms have a large range of technical terms, usually only a minority of words form the majority of the words in regular use. Research which words are the most heavily used (for languages, for instance, these are usually the same words in all tongues) in order to focus your memorising where it will have the most effect.

do the two numbers have to add up to 100. The ratio may be more like 60:10 or 90:5. The point is that a minority is responsible for the majority.

The 80/20 rule shows us that while we expect causes and consequences to be more or less equally balanced, in the real world they aren't. Of all the contributions made to getting a result, most will be of trivial importance, while a few will be vital. Therefore, by identifying the minority of factors which account for the majority of results, we can more efficiently deploy our memory skills. The 80/20 law highlights the importance of focusing.

So how does all this relate to memory?

The majority of memory mistakes result from the minority of bits of information

With any given list or range of items you have to memorise, it's likely that when you test yourself you'll find that the same few items each time give you the most trouble. Identify these few key hard-to-remember items as quickly as you can and focus your efforts on them. It may be that the technique you are using to remember them isn't working, so try another, or try modifying your method. Also, simply try repeating these few pieces of information over and over until you can remember them with ease.

The majority of information isn't worth memorising

We naturally forget most of the information we encounter in everyday life – for a good reason: most of it is unessential. Therefore, it's not worth worrying too much about not being able to recall trivial things; concentrate your energies on the few things which are worth memorising instead, and memorise them well.

The key to understanding anything seems to be to simplify it and identify a very small number of powerful causes.
RICHARD KOCH, author of *The 80/20 Principle*

Defining idea...

Even when you have to memorise a body of information, prioritise its individual elements first. Which bits are the most vital for you to memorise, and which are the least important ones? Start by revising the most vital ones, then work your way down.

A minority of facts will help trigger a majority of the information you need

Typically, only a small number of pieces of information are needed to trigger your memory for all the facts within a particular field, just as you may only need the titles of ten tracks to remember a whole album's worth of song lyrics. These are like the index references. In order to identify these small number of 'trigger' facts, first spend some time jotting down the organisation of the information you are trying to memorise. Build an overview map.

A minority of principles explain the majority of effects

If you are learning anything new, first ask this question: what are the core, the most important principles? Get an overview of the subject and try to grasp these core elements before you go on to grasp the details. These are often the very principles which you will need to understand in order to make sense of the rest of the information. Spending time learning these will be disproportionately valuable, as it will make learning all the other bits much easier.

How did it go?

Q   How do I identify the most important 20%?

A   *Honest observation. Start by asking yourself which memory techniques have worked the best for you, or which pieces of information you have the most trouble remembering. Also, ask an expert within the field you are studying what the most vital 20% or so of facts are.*

Q   What should I do about the less important 80%?

A   *Aim to minimise or even drop the time spent on the less important 80% in order to maximise the time you spend on the vital 20%. It's not always possible to completely ignore the less important elements, but you can almost always spend less time on them.*

25

A schedule for making memories stronger

Most information we take in through our senses is forgotten very quickly. If it wasn't, our minds would become overwhelmed with meaningless data.

So if you want to remember something long term, you're probably going to need to review it repeatedly. Follow this time plan to make a memory permanent.

Despite some cases where individuals appear to have retained an extraordinary amount of trivial information from their past, most memory experts believe that we don't remember everything. There is a mechanism which must be activated if a memory is to go into our long-term store. This chemical process seems to guard against us remembering unimportant details: it rarely encodes anything into memory if we only experience or think about it once. The best way around this is to review the information a number of times, with periods of rest between them.

A nineteenth-century German psychologist called Hermann Ebbinghaus discovered that forgetting follows an exponential slope: in other words, the sharpest drop in our memory of something occurs nearest to the time we experienced it, but then

Here's an idea for you...

Whenever you're learning something important, straight away plan to review it at least at intervals of a day, a week and a month later. Use a calendar or diary to plan out when you will review the material. Feel free to modify the schedule to fit your needs. For example, if you're revising for an exam in two weeks' time, then the month review will obviously not be needed, but you may want to review more in the early stages. Just use the general principle of organising the majority of reviews soon after you first encounter the information.

the drop-off evens out. This is basically true for everyone. However, there are three factors influencing variation from person to person: the difficulty of the material, how meaningful it is to us (for example, abstract information is forgotten more quickly than emotionally intense info), and our own state of mind at the time. What this means is that the first hours and days are the most important time for reviewing new information you want to remember in the long term. The longer you can remember something, the more likely you will be to remember it for even longer. The younger a memory is, the more vulnerable and weak it is. Imagine each memory is like a sickly newborn lamb: if you can just nurse it through its first twenty-four hours, then its chances of survival double; if you can nurse it through its first week, its chances double again, and after that it will only require attention now and then in order to survive.

To give a memory the best possible chance to be stored longer term you need to review it at least several times. A review can simply mean reminding yourself of the information, but ideally it involves testing yourself on the information you want to encode long term. Testing not only means you'll be thinking more deeply about the information (and hence more likely that you'll encode it) but it will highlight which areas you are most prone to forgetting, enabling you to pay special attention to them.

Here's a suggested schedule for reviewing information you want to store in long-term memory:

- one hour,
- one day,
- one week,
- one month,
- one season (three months),
- one year.

Voters quickly forget what a man says.
RICHARD M. NIXON

Defining idea...

There is one other barrier to encoding memories into your long-term store: a phenomenon that psychologists call 'interference'. Basically, this is when you confuse one piece of information with another. For example, if you were trying to learn German but had only just learned Spanish, then one of the two could interfere with your ability to recall the other. This problem is particularly bad when those two bits of information were experienced close to one another (such as trying to learn German and Spanish at the same time), and when the two types of information are very similar (German might be more likely to interfere with learning Spanish than sign language would). To avoid interference, try to avoid learning similar information close together in time. Also, just be aware of the potential for interference, and emphasise the differences between two similar things you need to remember.

After a meeting, or learning something new, make it a habit to quickly review the main details, such as the names of any new people you met and the main points that were decided upon. Then review the information an hour afterwards, and just before you go to bed that night.

How did it go?

Q **What if I review the material, but still forget it?**

A *It's almost certainly not the review schedule that is the problem here, but the way you initially learned it. Ask yourself the following questions. Do I fully understand the material? Am I studying it in a way that makes it most meaningful to me? Am I using good memory strategies to encode the material?*

Q **What if I find that I've forgotten the material before my first review at one hour?**

A *For particularly hard-to-remember material, feel free to review earlier than one hour, at – say – ten minutes, or even immediately if possible.*

Q **I have a lot of information I want to learn. Wouldn't having separate review schedules for everything just be too complicated?**

A *Set aside at least an hour, once a week, for reviewing all the information you want to remember. Keep a file, folder or notebook with this information in and base your weekly review on it. If there is too much information to review in depth every week, then simplify the recommended schedule by just reviewing information one week and then one month after you first learn it.*

26

Find the rhythm

Using rhythm and rhyme will really boost your memory powers.

Ever had a tune stuck in your memory all day? Irritating, perhaps, but rhythm, rhyme and melody are often overlooked as memory boosters.

Recite the alphabet in your head. Chances are that you 'hear' it in a certain way, with a certain 'sing-song' rhythm and melody. It's probably the way you were taught it at school, almost like a song. It's an extremely effective way to encode information into memory which otherwise might be hard. It also naturally breaks down the information into bite-sized chunks, making it easy for your memory to digest. So if it works for the alphabet, why not use it for other things too?

People have known for thousands of years that rhythm and melody are natural memory boosters. Epic poems and songs were encoded using this method. Before paper and books the only way to pass down large amounts of information, such as tribal wisdom, history and religious texts, from generation to generation was to tap into the memory-enhancing powers of rhythm. It also made the information more entertaining, as the elders sang the history of their tribe to the younger members around the flickering fire at night.

Here's an idea for you...

Try remembering one poem per week. Each evening, before you go to bed, repeat the poem several times. Start by learning the first verse, then the second, and so on. Then, each week, test yourself on the whole poem from the previous week. Remember that the rhythm and rhyme within most poems will be a natural memory aid.

If you think it's amazing that information the length of a whole book could be memorised in verse, think about your own ability to remember song lyrics. The chances are that you can, fairly easily, recall the words to tens or hundreds of entire songs. And that's a lot of words. All you need is the title or a little snippet of the melody and it will, typically, trigger off the whole song in your mind. You can probably also still recall with ease songs and nursery rhymes from your childhood.

Equally, the advertising industry knows the power of rhythm and melody to put information into our memories. Jingles, catchy little songs containing the advertiser's message and brand name, have been used on radio and TV for decades. They clearly work – and you've probably experienced this effect yourself, and cursed it as you can't get a jingle out of your head!

Music has a natural structure to it which, even if we aren't musically trained, makes it easy for us to remember. Another reason why songs are so easy to remember is that each line triggers the next. This is especially true when the words rhyme, as the end of one line suggests the kind of sound that must come at the end of the next line. Equally, the melody or rhythm plants clues as to what the next line or section must be.

You can make information easier to remember by injecting some musical qualities into it. You probably find you already do this, for example when remembering a phone number. If you repeat the phone number in your head, the chances are that there is at least a bit of a rhythm to it. You can take even longer numbers, such as your credit or debit card number (usually around sixteen digits), and remember them the same way. Simply break the number down into chunks of two to four digits, and repeat over and over, giving each chunk a slightly different intonation in your mind, or say it out loud (if no one is around). If you feel like being creative, you could try making up a short rhyme to remember a particular fact, such as a friend's birthday. Here are a couple of examples for historical facts:

In memory everything seems to happen to music.
TENNESSEE WILLIAMS

Defining idea...

- The Spanish Armada met its fate, in fifteen hundred and eighty-eight.
- In fourteen hundred and ninety-two, Columbus sailed the ocean blue.

You could even turn information into a full length poem or song, if you wanted.

It helps if the rhyme paints a vivid mental image. Also, with any of the rhymes you make up to help remember information, repetition is important. You may even like to make an audio recording of yourself and listen to it several times.

If you wanted to get really creative, and you had the time, you could devise alternative lyrics to a song you already know. Your new lyrics would encode the information you were trying to memorise, while fitting into the structure of the original tune. The educational TV series for children, *Sesame Street*, often used this technique. For example, in one case they took the Beatles' 'Let it be' and 're-imagined' it as an ode to the letter B.

How did it go?

Q **But I'm no good at music, can this still help me?**

A *Even if you aren't musically talented, and your singing makes small children cry, you can still use this technique. After all, you can still remember songs even if you can't sing them well.*

Q **I've got a lot of things to remember. This technique is just impractical for remembering big volumes of information, isn't it?**

A *It may be, depending on how much time you want to put into devising rhymes, and how creative you are. However, I'm not suggesting that this is the only memory technique to ever use, merely that it's one useful technique which may be appropriate for remembering small amounts of information.*

Q **What kinds of information does this work best with?**

A *Usually with single facts, and with long numbers. You may like to use it to remember all your friends' and family's birthdays, with particularly hard-to-remember facts, and all your essential numbers such as bank cards, car registration/licence number, bank account number, phone numbers, health or national insurance number and so on.*

27

Writing is not cheating

Just because you want a great memory doesn't mean that you shouldn't use notes too.

Geniuses do it, star students do it and the most effective business executives can be almost obsessive about it. Even in the age of computers, old-fashioned note-taking is just as useful as ever.

Jotting things down in a notepad may seem counter-productive if you are trying to boost your memory, but it's actually complementary to it. The chances are that you already take notes, just not in any organised or systematic way. I believe doing so can be an important part of the memory process: the very act of writing things down forces you to understand and organise them in such a way that they are then more easily memorable. For this reason, many of us find writing a useful learning technique in itself. Equally, there are many types of information which you might need to retrieve in the future, but are not so vital to everyday life that you would want to spend the time and effort memorising them. An example of this is information which may be useful to you at some point but you're not certain which bits you'll need, or exactly when you'll need them.

Here's an idea for you...

Keep a notepad with you at all times; you never know when you might need to jot down important information. A small pad that fits easily into a pocket is best. Most of the time, for most people, paper is still better than electronic organisers, as it's quicker to use, and you don't need to be so worried about it being stolen. Important long-term notes can then be transferred to a digital storage medium later.

Writing up your notes a day or week later will give you a vital review of the information, helping to consolidate it into your long-term memory. At this point you can choose whether to physically write them up using pen and paper, or whether to transfer them onto a computer. The advantages of typing up notes into a digital form are that they're easy to access from different locations (if you have them stored online), that you can easily make or share additional copies and, perhaps most importantly, that they then become searchable by date and keywords. Many note-taking applications also allow you to insert photos, clickable web URLs, sound clips and other add-ons to enhance your notes. And thanks to the continually dropping price of computer storage, and the continually increasing power of computers, there's no need to be stingy in how much you store; you'll probably never run out of space in the future. Equally, it's highly likely that computer search algorithms will increase in power and complexity, making it ever easier to perform more intelligent searches on your library of notes.

By making notes of things to follow up in future, we free up a lot of mental space, allowing us to concentrate better. Similarly, taking notes can be essential in writing to-do lists. Very little research has been done on how to improve our prospective memory, our ability to remember to do things in the future. While you can use list-memorisation techniques to accomplish this, there are two problems. Firstly, you may find that you get confused between a new to-do list and an old one. This is a particular danger if you use the same mental list system (e.g. a list of ten items) regularly but for different lists. The second drawback of memory techniques for short lists of to-do items is that they can almost be too successful: when you are trying to remember the list of grocery items you need to get in the shop this afternoon, you may still recall your list from last month.

The palest ink is better than the best memory.
Chinese proverb

Defining idea...

Students, in particular, need to take notes in lectures and classes. Even if they have well-trained memories, most will not want or be able to memorise things fast enough to keep up with the speed at which the teacher is speaking for a whole hour. This would be the equivalent to entering the world memory championships every day of your school or college life! You may like to try the Cornell note-taking method for students: divide your page so that there's a large margin at the bottom and down the left. After your classes, use the left margin to jot down the information in quick form, using key words. Then use the bottom margin to summarise the whole page in a couple of sentences.

Geniuses such as Leonardo da Vinci and Thomas Edison were prolific note-takers. Edison, for example, relied on his vast library of notes in his work life. During his lifetime he produced an astonishing five million pages of written materials. Even accounting for letters and other non-personally produced documents included in that figure, that's still a lot of notes. It's probably no co-incidence that Edison was both prolific in his work output and in the notes he took. By taking notes you don't lose information, or end up working on things only to realise you've repeated something you've already worked on. It makes you smarter, and more efficient.

How did it go?

Q **How do I stop losing my notebooks, or losing track of in which book I wrote something down?**

A *The answer is simple: you just need to organise your notebooks. Keep them together in one central location (feel free to place older, less regularly accessed notebooks into storage), keep separate notebooks for different themes or different projects or try colour-coding your notebooks (e.g. blue for meeting notes, white for creative ideas). Also, consider creating an index or contents list in each of your biggest notebooks to enable you to search them more quickly.*

Q **What should I keep notes on?**

A *Anything which is useful to you. This might include good quotes, recipes, creative ideas, future plans, notes on things you are learning, interesting dreams, sketches, newspaper clippings or notes from books you're reading.*

28

Personal restructuring

Make your own, completely personal, ways to order the info you are trying to memorise – and you'll be more successful at it.

Information can be like food: you need to chew on it well before you swallow.

Not only will understanding information make it easier to remember, but restructuring it in your own unique way will help even more. Each new memory has to be slotted into your brain, which is full of previous memories and associative links between concepts. The better able you are to link and associate the new information with what you already know, the more likely you are to remember it.

Whenever you are trying to learn new information, ask questions like these:
- What is this similar to that I already know?
- How could it be explained differently?
- What is the one over-riding principle which explains the most about this information?
- If I had to build an exhibit that explains this information, for a museum or conference show, what would I build? How could I build a model that explains or dramatises this information?

Here's an idea for you...

Try explaining whatever it is you're trying to learn to someone else. The very act of having to explain it will force you to make sure you understand it clearly. Also, the act of explaining it in your own words will help you to restructure the information in a way that makes most sense to you. Try explaining it out loud to a person, then try explaining it in writing to someone else. Finally, try explaining it in such simple language that a twelve-year-old child could grasp it.

- Who originated the information? What was their social, historical and philosophical context? (Where information originated often heavily influences its structure and assumptions, and can help you understand it better.)

As well as asking questions about what you are learning, it can also be useful to ask yourself how you learn best. There are many different ways to learn, and some of them will almost certainly be more to your taste than others. By taking in information via your preferred method you are more likely to learn it well. For example, if you find reading a chore, you might take in the same information better if it were in an audio-book format, or you might learn better with a group of people in a classroom environment than on your own.

You don't even necessarily need to restructure the information in a way that's unique to you, just so long as you've gone through the process of structuring the information. For example, the image in a jigsaw puzzle is not defined by you, it already exists. But you have to piece it together yourself. Equally, most bodies of information do have their own, natural structure or system of rules, but which aren't always immediately apparent. Through the process of studying material, you may eventually have an 'ah-ha!' moment when you finally realise the principles by which the information is structured. At that point it is worthwhile to stop and rethink what it is you are learning.

Information is alienated experience.
JARON LANIER, computer scientist

Defining idea...

In fact, the act of finding the structure of information is now known to actually affect where in the brain we process it. The top part of the brain, the cortex, is about the size and thickness of six napkins, one on top of the other, all scrunched into your skull (which is why, if you look at an image of the brain, it has many folds on its surface). The cortex can be divided into left and right 'hemispheres', which, in the past, have been described as being creative (the right hemisphere) and logical (the left). Neuroscientists now treat this description of the two sides of the cortex as a gross oversimplification. One new theory of the two differences is that the right side of the cortex is more responsible for processing novel information, while the left is responsible for processing information for which we already understand the rules and structure. Brain-imaging studies seem to support this. Basically, when we first begin to learn new information that we don't understand, our right brain plays a greater role than the left. Then, once we've decoded its structures, the activity shifts more over to the left side. For example, most people process music using their right hemisphere, but trained musicians, who understand the structure of music, process it more with their left hemisphere.

How did it go?

Q **The information I'm trying to learn is basically meaningless – like phone numbers. How do I relate this to what I already know?**

A *You need to decide whether this information really belongs in your head or in a notebook, diary, PDA or other external device. If it's meaningless, then the assumption should be that you shouldn't waste your time memorising it and it would be better recorded in an external device. The only exceptions to this are high-priority things, like your car's registration number or emergency phone numbers which you might feel are necessary to memorise. In these cases you will need to make an imaginative link between the number and some visual imagery, or repeat the number many times to burn it into your memory.*

Q **I've tried to find the structure to what I'm learning, but I'm struggling with it. Any more tips?**

A *Often, information is made more confusing than it needs to be because people are pushing their own particular agenda with it, trying to push their own structure onto it either because of their political views or because it is more convenient for them – for example, to try to sell you their particular 'method'. If you are stuck with finding the natural structure for something, consult a disinterested expert who does not have a method to sell or a political viewpoint to push. If this is impossible, then survey a few different experts.*

29

Don't slip off the learning curve

Learning is for life, not just your school years.

Why should learning stop just because you're an adult?

Many of us subconsciously assume that learning ends the day that we walk out of school or university for the last time. Yet as the pace of life increases, it becomes more valuable than ever to keep learning. For example, it can be important to your career to keep up with new technological advances, whether it's new software packages to master, new working practices to implement or new trends to adapt to. Also, many people are retiring at a later age than ever. A longer working life means that post-school learning becomes essential in order to keep up.

Another reason why lifelong learning is now so important is the demise of the 'job for life'. Very few people now enjoy permanent job security and business experts advise everyone, even employees of big organisations, to view themselves as though they were self-employed. This means taking responsibility for keeping your skills up to date. For many of us, the routine of our work can give a false sense of comfort which leads us to view our jobs as more secure than they actually are. Ask yourself: if you had to apply for a new job tomorrow, what would you apply for, and would

Here's an idea for you...

Consider signing up for a part-time class at a local college. Don't let any bad memories of school classrooms put you off; most adult evening classes are far more informal and fun. Plus you get to choose what you want to study. Who knows, not only will it stimulate your mind, but it could give your career a boost. Think about what subjects you always wanted to study, but perhaps felt were too frivolous or complicated.

your skills, as listed on your CV, make you stand out against other candidates? If not, then it's time to update them.

Knowledge is constantly growing. The amount of published material (both printed and online) is growing exponentially, as are new findings in science, as are new technologies. This not only means that a full education in many science and technology fields can now take longer than ever, but that if you are in one of those fields, you'll need to learn constantly in order to stay on track. Equally, the development of the Internet, and digital media like DVDs, MP3s and CDs, means that it's easier than ever to learn things at your own pace, in your own time.

It is true that it can be easier to learn new things at a younger age. For example, it may be easier for most people to learn a second language when they are a child than as an adult. This doesn't mean that it's impossible, just that a younger child will absorb the language with less effort. However, your brain is not hard wired during your youth. New findings in neuroscience have revealed how 'plastic' the brain is: it can remould itself. For example, when one region of the brain is damaged, it's possible for other regions to take over. Different tasks are not necessarily fixed to certain positions within the cortex. Equally, it's no longer possible to predict exactly what skills someone will need when they are a child. During the early industrial era, it was possible to plan universal education programmes on the basis that a certain set of skills would see each person through to their retirement, which meant that the only education most people needed was during their childhood. This is quite clearly no longer the case, yet we still hold to the notion that education is something for the young.

> *Never grow up, but never stop growing.*
> ARTHUR C CLARKE, science fiction author

Defining idea...

Constant learning is a great way to keep your memory strong in old age. Research has shown that the more memories a person builds, the more resilience they will have to any mental decline in their later years. Being a lifelong learner can also mean being open to novelty, to be willing to 'unlearn' previous memories. If we have invested years of our lives in doing things one way, it's difficult to overturn those habits and adopt a new way. But if you can overcome any resistance to this when it's wise to, then you will have developed a mental flexibility which will serve you well in all areas of life.

Remember, when learning new physical skills, be they touch-typing or skiing, research shows that a good night's sleep will help your brain encode these new memories. This may be particularly important for older adults, who tend to get fewer hours of sleep than younger people. Equally, even if you are not that old, you may still be cutting back on sleep due to a busy work schedule. Make time to get enough sleep. It's an important factor if your brain is to operate at peak efficiency.

How did it go?

Q **I accept the importance of lifelong learning, but I've no idea where to begin. What should I do?**

A *Make a list of skills you've always wanted to learn, or fields of knowledge you'd like to master. Now decide what your main aims are: do you want to learn something which will be useful to your career, or more as a personal interest? Then compare the two lists. Which items on the first list also meet your learning aims?*

Q **There are so many new things I could learn, how do I know which skills will be most useful in advancing my career?**

A *Look at the job ads for positions you would like to apply for if you were changing jobs. What skills do they ask for? Then talk to people who hire in the job area you aspire to join about what they are looking for. Which skills do you lack that are in demand?*

30

The memory secrets of the parrot

Sometimes good old-fashioned repetition has its benefits...

...particularly if you follow these techniques.

Imagine a dense forest. One day you beat a path through the trees. It's slow and hard work but the next day, when you take the same route, it becomes a little easier as you push back more of the branches. Gradually, day by day, a clear footpath emerges.

Learning is a lot like that: repetition gradually strengthens your memory pathways. The more times you travel the same routes, the stronger the memory gets. If you only experience something once, and don't think about it again, it will almost certainly be forgotten.

Schools have now de-emphasised rote learning in favour of making sure students actually understand the material rather than simply memorise it. This has probably been influenced recently by the fact that the Internet makes it easy to look up facts – some people assume that carrying them around with you in your brain is now less important. However, some information, like the alphabet, foreign vocabulary or mathematical formulae, don't always have that much 'meaning' to them; you just need to be able to recall them quickly. Having them memorised, and always

Here's an idea for you...

If you've got the time and willpower, large amounts of text can be memorised by the shear force of repetition. Start off by reading the first one or two sentences, then look away or close your eyes and try and repeat them. Look back to the text and see how accurate you were. If you were unable to repeat the sentences, read them again, then try again until you can. Then add a couple more sentences in and try to repeat them all. Continue this process, accumulating longer and longer stretches of text in your memory.

accessible to you, offers benefits that looking them up does not. For example, you can access your memory more quickly than you can look information up. Also, by having information in your memory, you'll make it easier to learn more as you can associate new information with what you already know.

There are several research findings that can help to boost the effectiveness of your reviews, so let's look at them.

Don't just glance at the information in a shallow way

When most people think of repetition or rote learning, they assume that you are just repeating the information over and over. However, just re-reading or repeating the information is not going to be as powerful as processing it at a deeper level. For example, try to relate the information to things you already know, or each time you rehearse the information, try to come up with a metaphor that you might use to explain it to people. You can practise actually using the information, too. If you are learning vocabulary, try using it in different sentences, rather than just repeating it. If you are learning maths, try some different calculations to practise.

Vary your repetition

Repetition needn't, paradoxically, be boring. Your memory will be enhanced if you repeat the information in a different way each time. For example, one time you might read it, the next write about it, the next explain it out loud to someone or draw an illustration to explain it. On each repetition, come at it from a different angle.

Much can often be learned by repetition under different conditions.
ARCHER J. P. MARTIN, Nobel prize-winning chemist

Defining idea...

Only learn one physical skill at a time

Physical skills, such as those involving movement and co-ordination, like touch-typing, driving or skiing, benefit particularly from repetition. Practice, as we all know, makes perfect. However, when learning this type of skill, you are especially vulnerable to forgetting it in the first six hours. During this period you mustn't try to learn any other physical skill or it will interfere with the first one, and you'll probably forget it.

Add breaks between your repetitions

Repeating things continuously, in one session, is not as powerful as adding in gaps between your repetitions, especially if the information is complex. When you are learning the information for the first time, use only short breaks between your reviews, but then gradually lengthen them. Eventually, the most powerful technique is to wait until you feel like the memory is very weak before you do your repetition.

How did
it go?

Q   But if I understand the information, do I really need to repeat it?

A   *Yes! There are all kinds of things you've probably understood in the past,
but can no longer recall. What use is that? Well, it's of some use, as you
will be able to understand the information the next time you encounter it
(recognition), but you won't be able to easily and freely recall it when you
need to.*

Q   I'm not revising for any exams. How can repetition help me?

A   *There are a lot of everyday pieces of information that you would benefit
by learning so well that you'll never forget them, and always have them
instantly to mind. For example, think of a word that you always have
trouble spelling. Check the correct spelling, write it out and spend five
minutes just repeating its spelling over and over. Five minutes, non-stop.
Then break for ten minutes, and spend another minute repeating the
spelling. Then break for an hour and spend another minute repeating its
spelling. Finally, spend another minute repeating its spelling twenty-four
hours later. You've now almost certainly burned it into your long-term
memory.*

31

Make it real: concrete not abstract

Turn abstract info into something more concrete and it becomes more memorable.

Why is it more common for people to fear plane crashes than heart disease, even though, statistically speaking, you're far more likely to be killed by the latter than the former?

The grisly answer is that most of us find it far easier to bring to mind an image of a plane crash than an image of heart disease. Our memories are highly dependent on our imaginations, and our imaginations are highly dependent on our visual sense. Things that are hard, even in theory, to visualise, are (in general) harder to remember. Therefore, if you are trying to remember abstract information, it can be very useful to first translate it into something more easily visualised.

For example, a concept like 'hunger' is not automatically easily imagined, but if you turn it into an image of a man holding his stomach, with a miserable expression on his face, looking into an empty kitchen cupboard, it becomes far easier to bring to mind.

Here's an idea for you... **Study book covers, particularly novel covers, to see how the cover artists illustrate the abstract themes or concepts of the book in an explicit graphical form. The simple ones are usually the most powerful. Graphical signs are also good examples of how artists are able to turn concepts into images.**

However, it's not only things that we visualise that are more easily brought to mind. If you ask someone 'Are there more words which begin with the letter "R", or with that as the third letter?', most people will answer there are more that begin with R, even though this is not the correct answer. This is because we typically pay more attention to a word's first letter than its third (indeed, this is how we organise words alphabetically in the dictionary). Most people can far more easily bring to mind words that begin with a particular letter than those which have that letter in the third position. The first letter also disproportionately influences the sound that the word makes; therefore, when we are imagining hearing various words, the first letter will be very important.

There are four main ways you can make abstract information more concrete.

Broaden your learning

Learn more about the specific sensory aspects of what it is you are trying to memorise. Ask: what does this look, smell, taste, sound or feel like? Of course, not everything has a smell, taste or sound, but almost everything has a visual appearance. For example, if you are learning biology, don't just read about the various processes that go on inside cells, seek out images, videos and animations of these processes. Sometimes this will give you an 'ah-ha!' moment as you finally understand the process in a vivid way. Also, try to get some hands-on involvement with the thing you are learning. This is usually the best way of all for turning abstract information into something more tangible and real to you. Not only will it add in the vital sensory aspects of the thing, making it easier to imagine, it will also give the information a personal context for you as it involves something you actually did in a particular location on a particular day, rather than something which you simply read about, for example.

Tell me and I will forget; Show me and I may remember; Involve me and I will understand.
CONFUCIUS

Defining idea...

Exaggerate

For information which is subtle and more abstruse, you can try exaggerating it to make it easier to remember. For example, to imagine two chemical elements reacting together, you could picture them as giant objects clashing together, causing loud, bright explosions. If you already have a visual image for your memory, try making it bigger, brighter, more colourful and exaggerate its most important features. For example, with a mental image of a genius, you might exaggerate the size of their head in order to dramatise a big and powerful brain.

Create metaphors

Orators, playwrights and novelists have always known that turning a concept into a dramatic, visual metaphor can make it powerfully memorable. If you are trying to remember something intangible, create a metaphor for it that is easy to picture. For example, one metaphor I found useful when visualising the gravitational fields around planets was to picture various-sized balls on a large rubber sheet. The heavier the ball is, the more it will distort the sheet – just as a gravitational field distorts space–time around a planet – and the faster any other smaller ball near the distortion on the sheet would roll towards it (just as a smaller body entering a planet's gravitational field will be pulled into it). A picture, as they say, is worth a thousand words.

General into specific

If information refers to some class of things 'in general', try to imagine a specific example. For instance, if you were learning some statistics or medical facts about a particular demographic category, such as 'older African-American men', pick a specific member of that group, such as the actor Morgan Freeman, to represent the group in your memory.

How did it go?

Q   Creating new visual images for everything I want to learn seems like a very time-consuming process. Isn't there any way to speed it up?

A   *If you are repeatedly working with a specialised area, you could always create your own 'visual language' for turning things into images. This would allow you to follow one or more set rules for turning concepts into images. For example, if you were trying to memorise the characteristics of something intangible like numbers, chemicals or viruses, you could imagine each one to be an animal, based on that animal's habitat and behavioural characteristics.*

Q   I'm just not a 'visual' person. Will this still work for me?

A   *Yes; as mentioned, it doesn't necessarily have to be a visual image, merely a concept which is more concrete or easily brought to mind. You can also involve your other senses.*

32

The mall of the mind

Most people know their way around their local shopping mall. Here's how to use this large slice of mental 'real estate' to remember things.

It's probably the most powerful memory technique you'll ever find.

The ancient Greeks and Romans used to visualise their great halls and temples in their minds in order to store vast amounts of information. Our modern equivalents of large civic buildings are shopping malls. If there is a mall you are familiar with, then you are probably already able to recall its basic structure, and the positions of many of its shops. This highly structured mental 'space' is now the perfect tool for memorising lots of information by associating it with various positions around the mall. The real trick here is to be creative in turning the various pieces of information into visual images which you will place around your mental mall. You then only need to walk through the mall in your mind in order to recall the information.

Think of one or several areas of information you would like to memorise. This could be things you are trying to revise for an exam, or information for your job or a hobby. In order to memorise them in your 'mental mall' you just need to turn each piece of information into an image, which you will then place at a specific location in your mall. Just make sure that you not only create an image which easily triggers that piece of information, but that you link it strongly to that particular area of your

Here's an idea for you...

Test and strengthen your ability to recall buildings and places. Think of how many buildings you can recall in detail. These can include previous homes, homes of friends or relatives, schools or shopping malls. Take a few minutes when you won't be disturbed, close your eyes and visualise walking through the building. The more you do this, the more you will strengthen your ability to visually recall buildings and places.

mall. One thing that helps with this is to organise the shops or areas in the mall by subject. Also you could order information by linking images together, perhaps by turning them into a story-like sequence.

For example, if you wanted to remember the names, in order, of America's presidents, you might create a distinctive image of each president and place him outside each shop along a route through the mall, or within one shop. To remember the first three presidents, you might construct something like the following imaginary story. Outside a clothes shop, someone is putting a tonne of dirty washing into a washing machine (Washington), and because all the clothes are going into the machine there's a man standing naked with just a fig leaf over him like Adam (Adams), then when all the washing is swirling around in the machine, they see a little miniature man trapped inside, like Tom Thumb (Thomas Jefferson).

Once you're comfortable with this system, and you've managed to memorise the basic layout of the mall and the positions of many of its shops, you can then go on to further structure it in such a way as to make it easy to store and recall the information you will place in it. For example, you could create 'zones' within the mall for holding different categories of information. For instance, you could mentally colour-code different regions or give them compass co-ordinates (e.g. the north wing). You can also structure your mental mall by the types of shops. For example, the gift or greetings-card shops could be used to store details of birthdays and anniversaries, the phone shop could be used to store phone numbers, food shops or restaurants could be used to store recipes. Book shops, in particular, lend themselves to this technique as they are already organised according to subject matter. The shops could also be used to store information on the actual goods they contain. For example, a music shop could be used to store a list of bands whose music you would like to buy.

Virtually since the dawn of civilisation, we have organised our world in part around the function of shopping. The mall is, at heart, just an ancient organising principle that hasn't outlived its usefulness. Perhaps it never will.
PACO UNDERHILL, retail anthropologist, from *The Call of the Mall*

Defining idea...

Putting in some preparation work on your mental mall will make the whole process easier. Schedule a visit as soon as you can, and walk around paying more attention than you usually would. Make notes if you feel it would help, or sketch out a map. Alternatively, some larger malls give away free maps, or have them displayed – which you could copy. If possible, take a few photos at key points on the route.

The beauty of this technique is that you can make it as simple or as complex as you like. At the most basic level you could just use the rough layout of the mall to store ten or so items in your memory. At the most complex, you could go into great detail with each shop, storing multiple lists at different points in the shop.

How did it go?

Q **What do I do if I don't have a local mall that I'm familiar with?**

A *Even though malls are perfect for these types of large mental spaces, you could also use any large structured space, such as a street of shops, a sports stadium, a library, supermarket or your workplace.*

Q **My local mall is just too large and complex for this to be practical. What can I do?**

A *You don't have to use the whole mall. For example, many larger malls have multiple floors. Try just using one floor to begin with, then build from there once you become more practised at this technique.*

Q **So many of the shops in my local mall keep changing, and even the layouts within each shop change. How am I supposed to keep track of this?**

A *There's no reason for you to keep track of any changes; you can just use the layout as it exists at the time you begin building your mental mall.*

33

The Major System

It can take a fair bit of preparation, but with this 300-year-old system you can build a huge mental storage space.

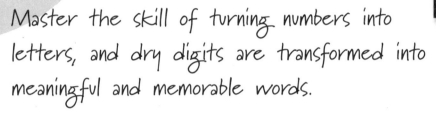

Master the skill of turning numbers into letters, and dry digits are transformed into meaningful and memorable words.

Turn those words into images and you've got a mental store of 100 compartments in which to remember anything you like.

OK, that might all sound a bit complicated, so let's take it step by step. The first thing you need to do is learn to associate each number with a consonant sound. Certain letters can have the same sound, like S and Z. This is why the Major System uses the sounds rather than restricting you to just one letter. However, the truth is that the actual number-to-letter coding system that you use is not important. You can even invent your own if you want, but here is the original (along with some tips for remembering it).

0 = S, Z (Z is the first letter of zero)
1 = D, T, Th (All these letters have one downstroke in them)
2 = N (N has two downstrokes in it)
3 = M (M has three downstrokes in it)

Here's an idea for you...

Build up your strength at using the Major System by practising it whenever you have some free time. The beauty of systems like this is that you can 'access' them wherever you are: standing in a queue, stuck in traffic or brushing your teeth.

4 = R (The last letter in four – yes, it is a slightly tenuous link, sorry about that!)

5 = L (L is the Roman numeral for fifty)

6 = J, sh, soft g (The number 6 can look like an upside-down lower-case g, or a mirror image of J)

7 = K, Qu, hard C (Turn your head sideways – to the left – and a K can look like the number 7 and a mirror image of it)

8 = F, V (When writing by hand, some people's lower-case 'f's look a bit like a figure 8)

9 = B, P (Lower-case b and p look like the number 9 rotated or in mirror image)

You then take the combination of the two numbers, and turn them into two consonant sounds. For example, if your number was 76, you would have the combination of K (or Qu, or hard C) and J (or sh, or soft g). By placing these two sounds or letters together, what word is suggested? It might be Cage. So 76 would then become associated in your mind with the image of a cage. Pay special attention to whichever word first pops into your mind with any particular combination, and consider using that association. If it's the one which you thought of first, it's likely to be the one you'll remember first. The whole aim here is to get to the point where any number between zero and ninety-nine will instantly trigger a picture in your mind.

Go through all the numbers between zero and ninety-nine (the numbers from zero to nine should be made into two-digit numbers by placing a zero in front of them) and decide on a word/image for every one. Again, this is time consuming, but it will pay off later.

You now have a mental filing cabinet with 100 spaces within which to store 100-plus bits of information. How do you store the information? Easy: you simply turn each thing you want to remember into an image, and link it to your number image.

A slight variation on the Major System has been developed by eight-times world memory champion, Dominic O'Brien. You might find the 'Dominic System' easier to use. It uses a number to letter system, like the Major System, but it's slightly different: 0 = O, 1 = A, 2 = B, 3 = C, 4 = D, 5 = E, 6 = S, 7 = G, 8 = H, 9 = N. Then every pair of letters is turned into a person and the action most closely associated with them, by thinking of what initials those two numbers/letters remind you of most. For example, 33, which would be CC, might make you think of Charlie Chaplin. And your image would be Charlie Chaplin dressed as the tramp character, swinging his walking cane. The beauty of this system is that once you've mastered it, it's pretty easy to remember four-digit numbers by using the image of the person from the first two digits, with the action from the second two. For example, if we had 8633, i.e. HSCC, we might think of Homer Simpson (HS) swinging a walking cane (CC – Charlie Chaplin's action). So, unlike the Major System, which is suited to 100 numbers, with the Dominic System you can easily go up to 10,000!

The Dominic System can also be used to remember phone numbers, by bunching the numbers together into pairs or fours. You can then make a mental story about the people and actions that the numbers suggest. A story which evokes strong images is way more memorable than a list of numbers.

The problem with numbers is that they are cold and unfeeling. But group a list of letters together and you have a word that represents an image, an emotion, a person. Throw a few numbers together and you have, well, another number.
DOMINIC O'BRIEN, eight-times world memory champion

Defining idea...

How did it go?

Q I just can't remember the letter associations with each number. What can I do?

A *Be persistent, and keep practising. Check that your associations are things that can be easily turned into mental pictures, and are not just words for abstract concepts. Are you having particular problems with certain numbers? If so, see if that number evokes any other strong associations in your mind. For example, the number ten might make you think of the British Prime Minister (10 Downing Street), or seven might bring to mind James Bond or Snow White and the seven dwarfs.*

Q I can remember the image for the number, but not the information I'm associating with it. How can I get that?

A *Try making the images more potent by making them more bizarre, emotionally charged, larger than life, comical or outrageous.*

34

Learning languages

Learning languages is hard, let's face it. But here's a way to boost your vocab with less effort.

The bad news: no memory technique is going to magically enable you to speak another language perfectly. The good news: some knowledge of how memory works can definitely help.

For most of us over the age of ten, learning a new language can be difficult. Children seem to pick up second languages more easily, particularly if they are spoken in the home. Research shows that we are indeed more able to pick up languages at a young age. But if you're an adult struggling with a foreign language, not all is lost. Knowledge of some basic memory techniques can help you, although they won't perform miracles, nor take away the fact that you'll still need to put in some hard work and many hours to master the language.

Firstly, consider what your goal is. Do you want to be able to pass yourself off as a local, or just grasp enough of the foreign tongue in order to function well on holiday? If it's the latter, then you could just use some memory techniques to

Try listening to a radio station in the language you are learning. Many radio stations can now be accessed online. By listening regularly you will be subconsciously absorbing the language in its everyday form. Vocabulary, rhythm and pronunciations will become more familiar to you. Vocabulary and pronunciation that you had been explicitly trying to learn will be repeated, meaning they are more likely to be encoded into your long-term memory.

memorise a handful of useful 'stock' phrases such as, for example, 'thanks very much', 'please may I have...' and 'how much is this?' It's amazing how far you can then get with just a few phrases mixed in with lots of gesticulating and pointing! Also, the locals will almost certainly appreciate even modest efforts to speak their language and will more than likely meet you half way if you make some effort.

So, take a piece of paper and write out the phrases you'd like to be able to say, and look up their equivalents in the foreign language. Also, make sure you know what the correct pronunciations are. There are two techniques you can use to burn these phrases into your memory within twenty-four hours. Firstly, repetition. Simply repeat out loud, and/or write each phrase over and over. Do this a few times, then take a ten-minute break and do it again. Take an hour break and do it again. Finally, do it again at the same time the following day. You can also use mental imagery. Take any key words from your foreign phrase and connect them with incongruent images relating to the meaning of the phrase. For example, in Spanish, 'What's your name?' is '¿Cómo te llamas?' So to remember this, you might think of a llama (llamas), reading *Cosmo* magazine (como) and looking up at you as you ask her name. Also, sometimes foreign phrases can sound very close to related English words (unsurprising, since languages are related to each other). For example, the Spanish for 'How much is it?' is '¿Cuánto es?' which sounds to me like 'Count it?' These associations can help you to recall phrases, but ultimately they are a supporting technique to practising them.

> *He who does not know foreign languages does not know anything about his own.*
> GOETHE

Defining idea...

The same principle can be used to memorise a list of fundamental vocabulary. Below is a list of the top twenty-five most-used words in the English language (which account for about a third of all written English; although, of course, this might vary with other languages), followed by another five words/phrases which you might find most useful when travelling. This list is just to get you started, and you may want to add in some words of your own too. As most of these words are simple, it may be hard to form mental imagery for them, so you will need to use plenty of repetition to master the list. Use the pattern recommended earlier (break after ten minutes, then an hour, then a day). When you test yourself on the words, make a note of which ones you get wrong most often and spend some extra time repeating those.

The	Is	For	They	Food or eat
Of	You	On	I	Drink
And	That	Are	At	Shop
They	It	As	Be	Where is...?
To	He / she	With	This	How much is
In	Was	His / her	Have	this?
			From	

How did it go?

Q **These memory techniques are great for simple uses of a language, but what if I want to master it at a greater depth and proficiency?**

A *There is no substitute for practice. Try to visit the country where the language is spoken and interact with native speakers. If you are unable to do this, try to interact with native speakers local to you. For example, join a language class or get a tutor if you can afford it.*

Q **The language I'm learning has different 'genders' for words. How can I remember them?**

A *Memory master Dominic O'Brien has a good technique for this. He recommends placing your mental imagery for masculine and feminine words in two different geographical regions you know well.*

35

Keeping your memory in old age

Maintain a masterful memory in your mature years.

People always assume that memory deteriorates as you age. It's very common to hear people complaining how bad their memory is and putting it down to their advancing years.

But is this an inevitable process? Well, mental abilities, including memory, can weaken with old age, but not necessarily as much as you might think, and there are things you can do about it. Thinking speed, attention and short-term memory abilities can all decline in old age, but wisdom can increase due to a larger memory store. A lot of what we do when we are 'thinking' is actually pulling up solutions from our memories, rather than working them out from scratch, and older people have a wealth of solutions from their past to draw from when faced with problems that could take a younger person more effort to resolve. The memory of a young person is like a small library staffed with a very fast and energetic librarian. The memory of an older person is like a vast and rich library, but staffed by a slower and less energetic librarian. But sometimes the 'tortoise' brain of the older person can beat the 'hare' brain of the young.

Here's an idea for you...

If you haven't had one in a while, make appointments for your eyes and ears to be tested. As we age, many of us experience a drop in the sensitivity of our sight or vision. Obviously, in order to remember things, we have to input them properly to begin with, so if you feel your memory has been getting worse with age, maybe you just need new glasses or a hearing aid.

The range of experience that an older person has access to can enable them to operate at a high level in competitive fields. Mathematician Norbert Weiner, writer Johann Wolfgang Von Goethe and philosopher Bertrand Russell all made important contributions to their fields in their more mature years. In politics, Winston Churchill, Ronald Reagan and Nelson Mandela are just three of the leaders who led their countries while in their seventies. Although they may not have had the mental speed of a younger person, they did have a lifetime's wealth of experience behind them.

The more intellectual skills and memories you've built up, the less hard any age-related mental decline will hit you. Imagine that your brain is like a large tree, which gets pruned back a little more each year as you move from middle to old age. The bigger the tree is to begin with – the more memories and intellectual strength you've built up – the less affected it will be by the pruning. Keeping your brain active can really help your memory in old age. Constantly aim to learn new things. Your retirement years can be a great time for pursuing interests which you never had the time for before. As well as learning new things, try new routines and new ways of thinking. Getting stuck in a routine is detrimental to your memory skills.

Also, in recent years, scientists studying the brain discovered that we can actually grow new brain cells throughout our lives. Previously it was assumed that we are born with all the brain cells we'll ever have, and that they start to die out from there onwards. However, after fifty the brain does start to shrink, but this doesn't mean all is doom and gloom. Keep stretching your mind and you will help stave off the effects of ageing to some degree. Also, research suggests that new experiences, and learning new information are key to memory-improvement exercises. So, as well as keeping your mind active with puzzles (such as crosswords and Suduko), learn new things, travel or learn about foreign cultures, improve your computer skills or do any activity which challenges you to think in new ways.

When I was a boy of fourteen, my father was so ignorant I could hardly stand to have the old man around. But when I got to be twenty-one, I was astonished at how much he had learned.
MARK TWAIN

Defining idea...

Set up systems to remind you. Use a calendar, diary and notepad. Pin important reminders on a pinboard in your home. Recent tests with elderly people taking many digital photographs during their everyday activities found that these were a powerful trigger for remembering. As taking lots of photos with a digital camera is now relatively cheap (once you've bought the camera), you may find this a good idea. Simply take lots of photos of activities you do, and organise them according to dates. You then have a visual record of where you've been and what you've done which will act as a great support to your memory.

You can also help your memory in old age by staying healthy. There's no big mystery to the things you need to do in this area: reduce your stress levels, eat a healthy, balanced diet and take regular exercise.

Evidence also suggests that your attitude towards ageing can actually have an affect on your memory. If you believe it's inevitable that your memory will decline, then that can become a self-fulfilling prophecy. Banish bad beliefs about memory, such as 'you can't teach an old dog new tricks'. Remind yourself that your brain can continue to grow new cells, and that in your more mature years you may have superior judgement and problem-solving skills due to your larger memory stores.

How did it go?

Q **Are brain-training video games better than paper-based puzzles at keeping the brain active in old age?**

A *There's no evidence to show that. What's important is that you actually challenge your brain, and do so regularly. Whether that's using computers, game consoles or by doing the puzzles in the newspaper is simply a matter of personal choice.*

Q **All this exercising and puzzle completion sounds like hard work. Isn't there anything easier or more pleasant I can do to keep my memory strong?**

A *There are no short cuts; physical and mental exercise are essential. However, as a reward for completing those, I'll reveal to you that new research has shown that a moderate serving (one glass a day) of red wine can keep your memory strong through improving circulation and preventing brain cells dying.*

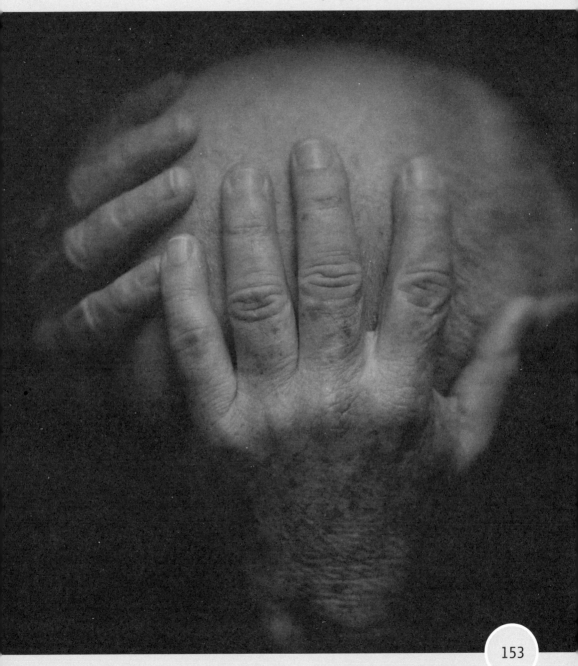

36

Make a mental memory vault for passwords

If you use computers and the Internet you will almost certainly have a list of user names and passwords to remember.

Here's how to do it in the most secure way; use this technique and within thirty minutes you'll have memorised all your computer passwords.

You'll also have tightened up their security, making it less likely that a hacker or identity fraudster could gain access to your accounts.

While the Internet, in many ways, relieves the burden on us to memorise things (we can just look them up in seconds), there is one case in which it puts more pressure on us to remember. In order to take advantage of the ever-expanding range of services online we often have to create an 'account'. When you create your account you typically have to provide a user name and password. However, it's best not to write these down anywhere, as there are plenty of people around who will steal them and access your accounts. This is particularly risky for Internet banking and any retail sites which store your payment details.

Therefore these passwords are the perfect candidate for items to memorise. You don't want to store them in a written form anywhere, yet at the same time you always need them to be instantly accessible.

The first thing to note is that it makes things much easier if you just have the same user name for all your accounts. Your security should reside in the password, not the user name (which is usually visible when you type it in anyway, whereas the password is usually blanked out as you type it). Also, many sites require that you use your email address as your user name, meaning that it won't be secret anyway.

In order to memorise your passwords we're going to use the technique of remembering a list of eleven items. There are two versions of this: the sound system (which uses images of things which sound like each number) and the appearance system (which uses images of things which look like each number).

Number	Sound system	Appearance system
Zero / 0	Hero (e.g. Superman)	Sun
One / 1	Gun	Pen/ pencil/ candle
Two / 2	Shoe	Swan
Three / 3	Tree	Handcuffs
Four / 4	Door	Sailing boat
Five / 5	Hive (i.e. beehive)	Curtain hook
Six / 6	Sticks	Elephant's trunk
Seven / 7	Heaven	Boomerang
Eight / 8	Gate	Snowman
Nine / 9	Wine	Balloon on a string
Ten / 10	Den	Bat and ball

Use whichever system you find easiest.

To memorise your eleven passwords, simply create an image for your password then associate that image with the image for the number. For example, for your first password (actually zero or o on the list), you will associate with either a hero (the sound system) or the sun (the appearance system). If your password was 'spaceship', then you might imagine a spaceship crash-landing into the sun, or Superman flying with a spaceship on his back. To make it even easier, you could add in an image for the particular account that the password was for. For example, if 'spaceship' was the password for your bank account, you might imagine a spaceship full of banknotes. If you need to memorise a longer list of passwords, then you can use one of the more complex systems, but eleven is enough for most people.

Once you've worked out your list, take a break for ten minutes and then test yourself. Then take another break for an hour and test yourself again. This will give you an excellent shot at getting those passwords into your long-term memory.

There are two golden rules when choosing passwords. Firstly, make them unconnected to you (don't use your pet's name or mother's maiden name). Most hackers are successful simply through assuming your password is something personally related to you. Most people only use something personal to them in order to make it easier to remember, but by using the techniques here that won't apply to you. Secondly, don't make them just letters, add in at least one number. This adds complexity, making your password harder to hack. To make this memorable, use the same number as its position in your list of eleven. For example, if your password was 'randomword', and it was the third in your list, you would make it 'randomword03'.

Here's an idea for you...

The big lie of computer security is that security improves by imposing complex passwords on users. In real life, people write down anything they can't remember.
JAKOB NIELSEN, computer security expert

Defining idea...

How did it go?

Q **I just don't feel 100% comfortable with relying entirely on my memory to store my passwords. Isn't there a secure way to back them up just in case I forget?**

A *Most Internet sites will allow you to reset your password if you really do forget. However, one way to back them is to make a series of little sketches on a piece of paper which remind you of your image associations for each password. This would be harder for any potential hacker to decode than a literal written list of your passwords.*

Q **Is there any way to remember an ultra-secure password?**

A *The hardest passwords of all to crack are those which aren't even normal words, but random letters and numbers. These are harder to memorise than word-based passwords, but it can be done. First generate a random list of numbers and letters. Then break them into chunks of three to make it easier to learn. You could easily then have a long password of nine characters made up of just three 'chunks'. Then repeat these chunks to yourself over and over, using some rhythm, as though it was a song. Test yourself an hour later, then a day later, and the chances are you will have memorised it.*

37

Create a learning wheel

Got a big load of info to memorise? Here's a good method.

When you're learning information in which one piece follows from the next, it's important to learn how they link.

The learning wheel is a technique for learning information in a sequence. It was devised by psychologist David Lewis, based on ideas by Gordon Pask. Pask was a British cybernetician and psychologist who worked on the idea that intelligence results from conversations and interactions, rather than something which only goes on inside our individual minds. It makes use of a number of core memory techniques, based around the idea of getting you to interact with information in order to learn it well: breaking information down into chunks, getting you to repeat information, giving you quick feedback on your results and, most importantly, strengthening the connections between pieces of information.

To create a learning wheel you're going to need a large sheet of paper, a sheet of card, some scissors and pens/pencils of various colours.

First, take your sheet of card and cut a hole in it, in the shape of a rectangle. Then, below that hole, cut a cross, then cut a rectangular flap that you can lift up or close. I've provided some suggested measurements below, but you can experiment with your own. This is your 'learning machine'.

Here's an idea for you...

Flashcards – blank postcard-sized cards which you can write and draw on – are a great way to summarise information you are trying to learn. Not only will the process of writing out the information help you memorise it, but so will the process of simplifying it in order to fit it on the card. If you find it hard to simplify the information, try breaking it down onto multiple cards, or try repeatedly writing out the information with fewer words, until only a small number of words trigger it all.

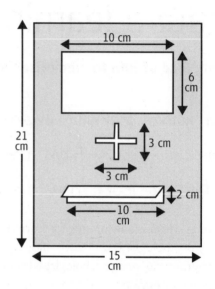

(Approximate suggested measurements)

Now, we're going to create your learning 'nodes', the spaces on the paper where you'll be writing the information you want to learn. Take your learning machine and place it on one top corner of your piece of paper. Use each of the three holes (the window, the cross, and the flap – opened up) as templates to draw onto the paper. The section that is revealed by the flap will be the top part of the next main rectangle (the idea is that the flap reveals the first line or two of the main rectangle).

With the cross, just make one line down (this is going to just lead you down to your next node). Then move the learning machine down, and draw your next node, and so on, until your paper looks like this:

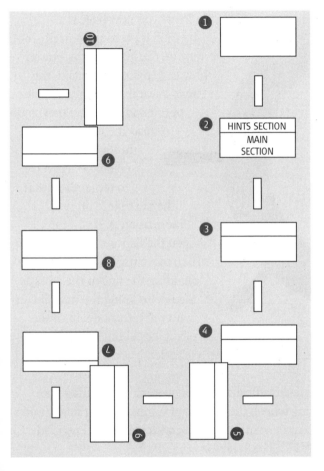

A wonderful harmony arises from joining together the seemingly unconnected.
HERACLITUS

Defining idea...

Note that when you get to the bottom or top of the page, you will need to move sideways, therefore you make a mark through the horizontal line on the cross, not the vertical.

Now, take the information that you want to learn – perhaps material from a textbook – and break it down into small chunks, equivalent to about a paragraph each. Each chunk should be based around one key fact. At the base of each node, in the space revealed by the flap, write a 'hint' as to what the next piece of information in the next node is. The next node will be information that follows on from the last one; there should be some kind of association or progression.

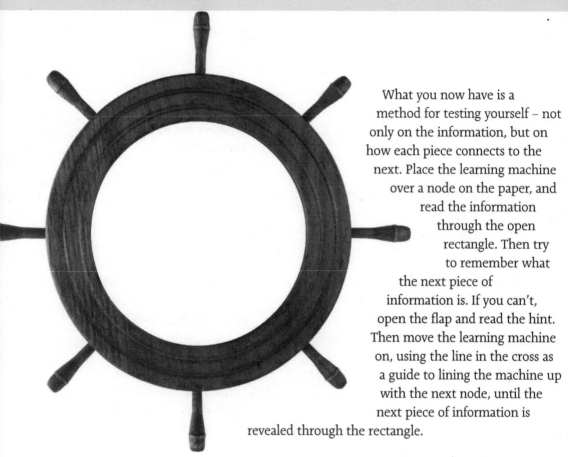

What you now have is a method for testing yourself – not only on the information, but on how each piece connects to the next. Place the learning machine over a node on the paper, and read the information through the open rectangle. Then try to remember what the next piece of information is. If you can't, open the flap and read the hint. Then move the learning machine on, using the line in the cross as a guide to lining the machine up with the next node, until the next piece of information is revealed through the rectangle.

You are already learning the material by creating your learning wheel; the process of summarising it into chunks forces you to think about it and understand it. Practise with your wheel regularly, testing your ability to accurately recall each node.

162

Q **I can't work out where I should start in the learning wheel, does this matter?**

A *No; vary the position where you start when testing yourself. The goal is to get to the point where any one fact can trigger the next and you can make your way around the whole wheel, from any starting position, without any mistakes. There is not necessarily any one official starting point. It's also worth mentioning that you might not always be able to get your last node on the wheel to connect to the first one, so you don't always have to have a complete circle.*

Q **How can I make this system more portable, or easier to use when I don't have much space?**

A *Instead of using a huge sheet of paper, you can use index cards or cut out each of your nodes from the paper so that you can carry them around with you.*

Q **Can I use the learning wheel to learn anything?**

A *No. It's not an appropriate technique with all information. For example, I wouldn't recommend using it with languages, or with 'non-sequential' types of information.*

How did it go?

163

38

Cueing and implicit memory

We know many things without knowing it; use the power of recognition.

Psychologists divide memories up into two types: implicit and declarative. Here's how to make the most of your implicit memory...

Declarative memories are the ones we can 'declare' or talk about. For example, if I asked you your age, the names of your parents or the word for a large, grey, four-legged mammal with a long trunk, they would be declarative memories that you'd be recalling. If, however, I asked you how you ride a bike or swim, you would probably have to think quite carefully and reconstruct the movements in your head in order to describe them.

These types of physical skills are an example of implicit memory: we've learned them without being able to consciously describe them well. Another type of implicit memory is for things we recognise. Put simply, we can recognise a lot more than we can recall. For example, you may be able to consciously recall the names of a few hundred people (both those you personally know, and those who are famous), but it's almost certain that you would be able to recognise many more numbers of faces if you were shown photos of them. In fact, there have been a number of fascinating experiments which have demonstrated this.

Here's an idea for you... **Learn to think like an author you admire. Physically copy out (preferably by hand, although you could type) a page of text by an author whose thinking you revere. Do this several times and you may start to absorb subconsciously their style and way of structuring information.**

The first, published in 1970, involved showing people 2560 photos over several days. They were then shown pairs of photos; one of each pair had been shown to them before, and one was completely new. They were then simply asked to identify which of the pair they had seen before. They managed to do this with, on average, an accuracy of between 85% to 95%. The experimenters then decided to test this further, and sped up the presentation of the images to one a second. The participants' accuracy was unaffected. Neither was it affected by showing them the photos in mirror-image format. Subsequent experiments tested people's ability to recall up to 10,000 pictures, and found similar levels of accuracy. Even more amazingly, one study tested people on images they'd seen in an experiment seventeen years previously. While hardly any of the participants could even consciously remember taking part in the original experiment, most of the images were recognised! Therefore, not only is recognition for images apparently almost infinite, it seems to be invulnerable to fading over time.

So it's easier to recognise than to recall from scratch when it comes to vision. In fact, our recognition memory is the closest thing we have to photographic memory; it seems to be almost perfect. The downside, of course, is that you have to be re-presented with the image in order to recognise it. Most of the time we think of memory skills in terms of being able to pull up from memory some information without being prompted. But if you can find ways to prompt, or 'cue' yourself, you can tap into this amazing strength of your memory. Also, psychologists believe this system works for our perceptions, images, sounds, etc., but not for concepts.

The best way to use this power is to enrich your environment with as many cues as possible. For example, try carrying a small inexpensive camera with you wherever you go, and take photos constantly of places you visit and people you meet. If possible, put a time stamp on these images too. This will give you a highly useful databank of images of your past to use as a memory prompt when trying to recall people or events. If you archive your photos on your computer, you will then be able to perform searches by date, to bring up photos for particular days or events.

Don't feel that you need to constrain yourself to always remembering things without any help, either. If you can consult a memory cue, such as a book, then do so. It may result in even more recollections than you would have been able to access had you constrained yourself to remembering unaided.

There are known knowns. There are things we know we know. We also know there are known unknowns. That is to say we know there are some things we do not know. But there are also unknown unknowns, the ones we don't know we don't know.
DONALD RUMSFELD, former US Secretary of Defense

Defining idea...

167

How did it go?

Q   What other ways can I use memory cues?

A   *Basically, take advantage of any sensory prompts that you can, whether it be looking at an image to remember more about an event or location or listening to a piece of pop music to remember more about the era when it was released. Also, trust your ability to recognise sensory information. Even if your conscious mind comes up blank, but you have the 'feeling' that something is familiar, trust the feeling and take a guess that you do recognise it.*

Q   Surely there must be limits to this? Why, for example, aren't people always spot on when identifying people in a police line-up?

A   *The problem with recognising a criminal from a line-up is that you may have tried to access the memory of the criminal's face many times since the crime, and this can interfere with your ability to recognise, particularly if you have heard other descriptions of the person. It can colour your memory. Therefore, if you wish to learn information using implicit memory, do so in a way that doesn't expose you to information which could confuse you. For example, if you are learning foreign vocabulary, don't test yourself on words until you are really certain you know them. Even wrong guesses could be recalled in future and confuse your implicit memory system.*

39

The coins in the pocket trick

A few coins can become a quick memory aid in any situation. Here's how to use memory props.

Sometimes it's helpful to use external props. You could jot things down in a notebook or, as inventors have done, on napkins. However, writing materials aren't always to hand.

And notes only really work if you remember to consult them again. If not, it can be counter-productive, as it can give you a false sense of security (because you've written the information down, you don't think about it again), mitigating against you remembering it. So, there are times when as well as using calendars, diaries and notebooks, you can use your own behaviour as a simple reminding system. There are two occasions when you can use these techniques to best effect.

Firstly, be vigilant when you are doing something repetitive or unconscious. Have you ever experienced driving to work, or on a long journey, and suddenly you realise that you've been daydreaming for the last ten or fifteen minutes and have no memory of driving? You may miss a turning or drive to work on your day off due to this kind of daydreaming. Psychologists call this effect commuter amnesia. When we can do something automatically, our conscious attention often wanders elsewhere. In some situations we must remain vigilant, but the monotony of the

Here's an idea for you...

If you have a short list of items to remember, use your environment to help. For example, if you are sitting at your desk, notice a handful of objects or visual landmarks around you. These may be things like a window, a computer, a pot plant, another person and so on. Make a mental, imaginative connection between each item and the thing to be remembered. Then, when you need to recall them, simply cast your eyes back over the objects as you recall each point in turn.

environment makes it hard. From the outside, it can be hard for people to see how difficult it is to keep attention up in those situations. Most people don't realise, for instance, that being a baggage security person in an airport is hard work. Equally, we may have goals in life which we wish to pursue, but because they are not pressingly urgent, we aren't prompted to do them – for example, to take regular exercise, relax more, smile more, meditate regularly. Amid the hustle and bustle of everyday life these things too easily fall through the cracks.

The cure for this kind of unconsciousness is to repeat a mantra word to yourself every so often. This might be something like 'focus', 'remember' or 'concentrate', but, in truth, the actual word you use doesn't matter so much as you simply repeating it regularly. The word will remind you to pay conscious attention to whatever it is that you need to. For example, say you want to remember to smile more during the working day. Remind yourself to silently repeat the word 'smile', either as much as possible, or at particular key intervals, such as on the hour, every hour, or every time you hear the phone ring.

Another solution is to use any portable device with an electronic alarm – like a mobile phone or a digital watch. You can then set this to go off at regular intervals during the day to remind you of whatever it is you need to pay attention to. Mobile phones are particularly good for this as they often have a 'silent vibrate' setting, which will allow you to remind yourself without other people noticing.

If you wish to forget anything on the spot, make a note that this thing is to be remembered.
EDGAR ALLAN POE

Defining idea...

Another time when you might want to use a memory prop is when you are in a situation where you would ideally want a notepad, but don't have one to hand. For example, you could be on the phone, having an important conversation, and it's vital for you to remember several pieces of information. Or you may be in a meeting, in which several key points are discussed, and it's essential for you to remember them afterwards. With no writing material, what should you do? There's a simple solution which relies on the fact that often, if you can just remember the number of things to be recalled, you will more easily be able to recall the things themselves. Simply keep a small number of coins (ten or less) in your pocket whenever you can. Begin with all the coins in one pocket. Then, when you are in your meeting or having your phone conversation, transfer one coin over to the other pocket each time a key point is mentioned that you want to remember. Afterwards count out each coin and try to recall each of the key points (and then write them down or rehearse them). You may find it a strain to remember all the points, but at least you will know if you haven't remembered them all. As you know the number of points you can keep thinking until you have remembered the lot. You can also use this technique if you have to remember a number of to-do tasks during the day, but you are unable to write a list. Simply put one coin in your pocket for each task to do, then transfer the coins over to the other pocket as you complete them.

How did it go?

Q   What if I rarely carry coins with me?
A   *You don't have to use coins; any small objects that you can carry in your pocket will do.*

Q   Are there any limits to this technique?
A   *Yes, it's only good as a memory prompt. It will remind you either of one specific thing (if you are using a mantra, like 'concentrate' or 'smile') or it will remind you of the number of things to do or to recall. It wouldn't be appropriate to try to use this technique to remember large quantities of information.*

40

Remembering directions

We don't always have maps or GPS to help us.

Here's where your memory can come to the rescue.

There are a couple of occasions when you're most likely to need to remember directions. The first typically occurs when you are lost. You stop to ask someone for directions (usually as a last resort), and suddenly a stream of directions issues forth from their mouth at such a rate that you lose track of what they are saying, and simply nod and smile politely. Unless you have writing materials or a map for them to point at, you are still lost – still, that is, if you don't use any memory techniques!

The first thing to note is the importance of paying attention when the person gives you the directions. Focus as intently as possible on what they are saying and tune everything else out. Then get them to repeat the directions.

Most directions are of the 'left, right, straight on, left...' variety. You can use a bit of repetition and rhythm to stamp them into your memory. For example, if the person tells you to go 'Straight on until the next left turn, then take the next right, then the next right after that, then go straight on and take the third left', this will become 'Left, right, right, straight, straight, left' (where you have a 'take the third left' you substitute with 'straight, straight, left'). If you then repeat this several times, bunching the words together into twos or threes and adding a bit of rhythm,

Here's an idea for you...

Create your own personalised maps on a computer or paper. Every time you visit somewhere new, mark it down on the map and take a few minutes to review other places you've been and the route used to get there. If you look at your personal maps regularly you'll be building a stronger internal map of where you've been, which will help in the future when you try to recall routes.

you will find it far easier to remember. You can also add any landmarks which are mentioned. So your repeated phrase in that case might be something like 'Left, right, right, church, straight, straight, mall, left'.

Research has shown that, in general, women are more likely to use directions of the 'left, right' and landmark variety, while men are more likely to mention compass bearings and distances. Be aware of which system you are more comfortable with, as this is the one you are most likely to remember. If someone gives you compass directions, and you are unsure of where north is, make sure you ask them to orientate you. Equally, you may like to stand side by side with your helper, rather than opposite, as they are giving directions – the reason being that it's very easy for them (or you) to get confused when giving 'right, left' directions. You may be trying to remember to go in the opposite direction than you should be.

The other occasion when you might need directions is when you are setting out on a journey and can't take a GPS or map with you. The advantage you have here is that you typically have longer to memorise the route than when you are asking for directions. Firstly, work out your route and simplify it down to the essentials, the turning points of the journey and the approximate distances. You can then use some basic mental imagery to memorise this list of directions. Try to keep your list of essential directions within ten (ideally, within seven). Then you can use the 'list of eleven' technique for memorising them. For example, if you were using a number-shape method (which turns each number into a visual image resembling the shape of that number, then pairs that with an image of the thing to be remembered), you might remember a list of directions as follows:

- ■ **1 – looks like a pen**. Drive until you reach the church then turn left (direction); imagine a giant pen on the left side of the church's cross (mental image).
- ■ **2 – looks like a swan**. Take the third turning on the right (direction); three swans jump onto the cross from the right (mental image).
- ■ **3 – looks like a pair of handcuffs**. Turn left at the school (direction), a schoolchild grabs the pen from the left of the cross, and puts handcuffs on the feet of the swans (mental image).
- ■ **4 – looks like a sailing boat**. Drive past the duck pond (direction), the swans turn into ducks on a pond, with a huge sailing boat stuck in the middle (mental image).
- ■ **5 – looks like a hook**. Turn at the police station (direction), the sailor on the boat throws his fishing line into the water, and when he pulls it up, there's a policeman attached to the hook (mental image).

If all that seems complicated, comfort yourself with the fact that it's only new directions that tend to be so hard to memorise. Routes quickly become familiar with use.

Just as nature abhors a vacuum, the mind abhors randomness... As naturally as beavers build dams and spiders spin webs, people draw maps, in the sky and in the sand.
GEORGE JOHNSON, author

Defining idea...

How did it go?

Q **I have a great ability to visualise, but a bad memory for directions. Is there any technique suitable for me?**

A *One technique you can use – either on its own, or in conjunction with the previous technique – is to visualise the route as a shape or a letter. For example, 'straight on, then right, then right' might be a lower-case 'n'.*

Q **What should I do if someone gives me really complicated directions and I just can't remember them?**

A *If the directions are so complex that you can't fully remember them even with this memory technique, then simply try to remember as many as you can. This will get you a lot nearer to your destination and then you can ask someone else for directions. Not ideal, but better than not remembering any of the directions.*

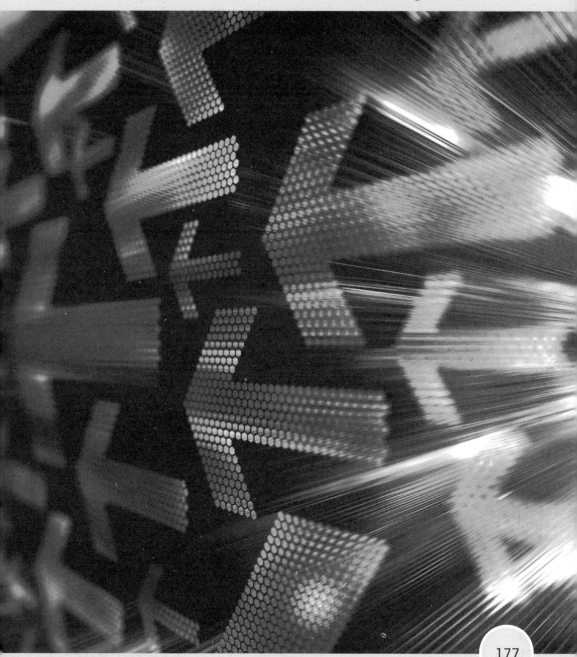

41

Remembering speeches and presentations

We may dread these more than death itself, but here's how to make them just that little bit easier.

One of the commonest nightmares is walking on stage to give a talk to an expectant audience, then suddenly realising you cannot remember a word you are supposed to say!

The nervousness that everyone feels (to varying degrees) about standing up in front of a crowd to talk can put our memory abilities under pressure. In fact, so few people are willing and able to give public presentations that those who can will find themselves able to command premium fees to talk to and for businesses and organisations and may find it a great asset to their career advancement. Therefore, firstly do anything you can to diminish your nerves as much as possible. Learn some breathing exercises, get some practice at talking in front of smaller groups before large audiences, and read some books on giving good presentations.

Once you've learned to calm your nerves, put some memory techniques to use so you'll remember your speech.

If you have a speech written out in full, first turn each sentence into a couple of 'prompt words' which will trigger the whole sentence or paragraph. Write out your prompt words, then test whether you can remember the whole speech just by looking at them. Once you've managed that, transfer your prompt words to a set of cards, which you can use as a backup in your presentation. A brief glance at each card should be enough to trigger at least a paragraph's worth of your speech.

Rehearse your talk

This may seem obvious, but many people want to avoid even thinking about giving the dreaded talk, so they skip this vital preparation. There are several reasons why it can be useful to rehearse. Firstly it helps to identify any areas of potential difficulty, such as hard-to-pronounce words. Secondly, the act of being rehearsed and prepared will give you more confidence when you stand up to deliver it for real. And, lastly, the very act of repeated rehearsal will help you to memorise what you are saying. Through repetition, you'll not only burn the content of the talk into your memory, but you'll be burning in the rhythm of your pronunciation of the sentences too, which, in turn, will help you remember your speech.

Summarise your talk into key sections

Break the structure of what you want to say down into key sections of up to about seven points. This has a couple of benefits. For one, it allows you to keep a mental track of where you are within your talk, something which can prove useful if you do happen to get lost or confused. It also enables you to memorise the talk in the first place, as you can give each point a mental image...

Give each section a striking mental image

Devise a clear image for each of your (up to seven) key points that is a powerful metaphor for that point, and then use each of those metaphors within your talk.

Images are not only the way your brain works best in terms of memory, but also in terms of communication and understanding. By creating some striking visual metaphors for your main points, your talk will come alive in the minds of the audience and they will be more likely to remember it too.

The human brain starts working the moment you are born and never stops until you stand up to speak in public.
GEORGE JESSEL, actor and public speaker

Defining idea...

Plan your speech according to the memories of your audience

People are more likely to remember the first and last things they hear. Therefore, assuming you want people to leave your speech with some memory of what you said, plan your talk around this fact. Give a preview of your key points near the beginning of the talk and then review them all at the end. Equally, people will only remember what they have paid attention to, so try to ensure that you state your key points clearly. Also, presentation slides should be simple enough to emphasise your key points without distracting people from listening to what you are saying.

Use environmental cues

Finally, here's a little trick you can use if you are able to get access beforehand to the location where you'll be giving your talk. Stand in the spot you'll be standing when you give your talk and look around you. Notice the main features of the room. These may be things like the lights hanging from the ceiling, windows, curtains, particular clusters of seating, etc. Next, associate each of your talk's key points with one of these visual features, in order from left to right (or right to left if you prefer) by making a visual link between that key point's image and the visual feature. Then, when you are standing up to give your talk, you can use these to prompt your memory for each key point.

181

How did it go?

Q **I will never give a speech in public. How can this benefit me?**

A *The same principles can be used even for talking in front of a small audience, such as you might have in a business meeting – or even in front of one person, if you are being interviewed.*

Q **Couldn't I just type my speech out and read it, rather than going to the effort of memorisation?**

A *The simplest solution to memory failure when giving talks – to just read, word for word, from a prepared script – is often unsatisfactory as it can sound unnatural and unengaging. Using some memory techniques to help you out will, therefore, improve your talk and allow you to concentrate on engaging your audience with more eye contact.*

42

How to become a date calculator

If you're an advanced memory maestro, here's how to tell any day of the week just from a date.

It's just perfect for impressing any adult with your ability to know what day they were born on!

This technique, developed by memory master Dominic O'Brien, allows you to work out which day any date in the twentieth century fell on. For this to work, you'll need to have mastered the ability to visualise an associative image for any number from zero to a hundred, be comfortable linking words to numbers and be well versed in using the rooms of your house to memorise images. You can do all that? OK then, let's begin!

Basically, we're going to memorise three number codes, which will then be used to calculate the date. Firstly, you will need a mental image (ideally of a person) for each of the numbers between 0 and 100. Each of these will then go after the prefix '19' to form one of the years of the twentieth century. Then you need to assign each of seven rooms in your house (or other building that you can visualise) a number between 0 and 6. Now, you are going to mentally place each of your people or objects into one of those rooms according to the code below. Obviously this will take some time and effort:

Room	Years:														
0 =	00	06	17	23	28	34	45	51	56	62	73	79	84	90	
1 =	01	07	12	18	29	35	40	46	57	63	68	74	85	91	96
2 =	02	13	19	24	30	41	47	52	58	69	75	80	86	97	
3 =	03	08	14	25	31	36	42	53	59	64	70	81	87	92	98
4 =	09	15	20	26	37	43	48	54	65	71	76	82	93	99	
5 =	04	10	21	27	32	38	49	55	60	66	77	83	88	94	
6 =	05	11	16	22	33	39	44	50	61	67	72	78	89	95	

In order to remember which of your rooms corresponds to each room number, you might like to place an object in each room that looks like that number (e.g. a plate for '0', a swan for '2'), or you could imagine walking through the rooms in the order of their numbers.

Next, you'll need to associate a number with each of the months:
April and July = 0, January and October = 1, May = 2, August = 3, February, March and November = 4, June = 5, September and December = 6.

Finally, you'll need to order the days of the week from Sunday to Saturday, assigning each a number: Sunday = 1, Monday = 2, Tuesday = 3, Wednesday = 4, Thursday = 5, Friday = 6, Saturday = 0.

Now you're ready to calculate your days.
- Take the date (the 1st, 3rd, 22nd – whatever), and subtract as many full sevens from it as you can, then write down the remaining number.
- Take the number for the corresponding month.
- Take the room number for the corresponding year.

Now add those three numbers together, and it will be equal to the day of the week. If your total number is greater than six, then simply subtract as many sevens from it as you can, and keep the remaining number. That's your day of the week.

Here's an example which will clarify things: Let's say someone was born on 1 May 1962. Which day was that?

- You can't take any sevens from one, so the answer is just 1.
- The number for the month of May is 2.
- The year 62 is in room 0.

Therefore we need to add 1, 2 and 0, which gives us 3. The day was Tuesday.

Here's another example: To work out the day for 8 April 1976:

- There's one seven in eight, so we take that out, and are left with 1.
- The number for the month of April is 0.
- The year 76 is in room 4.

Therefore we need to add 1, 0 and 4, which gives us 5. The day was Thursday.

If you are working it out for a date in January or February of a leap year (which is any year which is divisible by four) then you simply need to subtract one from your final answer.

Here's an idea for you...

Memorise the birthdays of your friends and loved ones. First, devise a mental image for each month (tip: use holidays such as Christmas, Halloween, Easter or traditional activities like August holidays, or back to school in September to suggest images for each month). Then choose images to represent the numbers from one to thirty-one to represent the dates. Now, simply create an imaginary scene in which your friend/family member is interacting with the image for that number, and with the month image (perhaps, if you've chosen a holiday image, as a background to your friend interacting with the date image).

Defining idea...

A diplomat is a man who remembers a woman's birthday, but never her age.
ROBERT FROST, poet

How did it go?

Q   Are there any more tips to help me remember the year and/or room code?

A   *Which room would you be in based on your birth year? What conversation or interaction would you be having in that room with the people or objects you've imagined there? Also, copy down the grid of year numbers and carry it around with you for a couple of weeks. Offer to work out the days people were born, then double check your grid to ensure you get the year-room correct. Many people may not actually know the day they were born on, so it will help to have some way to check you're on the right track!*

Q   Will this work on twenty-first century dates?

A   *I'm afraid not. But just knowing the twentieth-century dates will impress most people and, for the near future, be good enough for knowing the day on which most people were born.*

43

Using acronyms

A quick and easy way to remember a list of connected facts.

Got a list of words you need to memorise? Acronyms are a great aide-memoire for summarising information down into a bite-sized chunk that your memory can easily swallow.

Acronyms are words constructed by putting together the first letters of other words. They act as a way of summarising, and hence make those words more easily memorised. They're a relatively new phenomenon, only really taking off in the last fifty years and probably reflecting the development of scientific, technical and military fields in this time (as these are areas which are particularly fond of acronyms). The *Oxford English Dictionary* records the first use of the word in 1943. It comes from the Greek for 'topmost' (*akros*) and 'name' (*onoma*). Some people refer to acronyms which can't be pronounced as 'initialisms' or 'alphabetisms'. These are older, and date back to ancient Rome.

Examples of acronyms:
- SCUBA (Self-Contained Underwater Breathing Apparatus)
- LASER (Light Amplification by Simulated Emission of Radiation)

Here's an idea for you...

Ask someone who has already mastered the area of knowledge you're trying to learn if they've used any acronyms they found useful. Doctors, in particular, usually have lots of these. There may be some very useful acronyms for your area of knowledge but it's unlikely (particularly if they are ribald or politically incorrect!) that you'll find them in the official textbooks.

- NATO (North Atlantic Treaty Organisation)

Examples of initialisms or alphabetisms:
- USB
- BBC (British Broadcasting Corporation)
- IBM

Similar to acronyms and initialisms are sentence acrostics. Instead of turning the first letters of each word into one word, these involve turning the first letter of each word into another word, which forms a sentence. For example, 'Richard Of York Gave Battle In Vain' gives you the colours of the rainbow: red, orange, yellow, green, blue, indigo and violet. The advantage of this method is that it usually allows you to form a mental image, making it more memorable. You could also create your sentence acrostic in the form of a rhyme, further enhancing its memorability.

Creating an acronym is easy. Simply:
- Take the first letter of each word you wish to remember, and write it down.
- Shuffle the letters around until you can form them into a pronounceable word. I say this as it's usually not possible to turn the letters into a real word, so the next best option is to at least create a word which is pronounceable. NATO is obviously not a real word, but is perfectly easy to say. However, if you find that you are almost able to create a real word, except for one letter that doesn't fit, see if you can change that one word to another with the same meaning, but beginning with the required letter. Use a thesaurus to help you search for an alternative word. If you can't form a real word, or a pronounceable one, then you'll have to make do

with an initialism. This is not as good as a pronounceable acronym as it's not quite as memorable, although it will still work.

- Take a five- or ten-minute break and do something completely unrelated. Then come back and check whether you can still remember the acronym. This will expose any weak points in it, any letters you can't remember. Focus on learning those through repetition. Vary your repetition, so that you are speaking it out loud as well as writing it down.

The ability to simplify means to eliminate the unnecessary so that the necessary may speak.
HANS HOFFMAN, artist

Defining idea...

The disadvantage of acronyms is that they merely aid recall and not understanding. They help you to recall the words, but not necessarily the meanings of those words, or how to apply the knowledge in different ways. So you'll still need to put some time and effort into understanding the material, separate from creating the acronym for it.

To summarise, here are the three methods, in order of preference:
- **Sentence acrostics, the best system**. Benefits: can provoke a mental image, or be formed as a rhyme. Easily retains the order of words. Drawback: can take longer to create a good, memorable sentence.
- **Acronyms, the second-best system**. Benefits: If it's a real word, then it can be turned into a mental image. It's more memorable than an initialism. Drawbacks: doesn't rhyme, and doesn't always lend itself to mental imagery. Doesn't necessarily retain the order of words.
- **Initialisms, the least-preferable system**. Benefits: still allows you to summarise information, and make it more memorable than in its original form. Drawbacks: less memorable than a real sentence, word or pronounceable word. Doesn't necessarily retain the order of the words.

How did
it go?

**Q   I find it hard to form an acronym word out of the letters I have.
Any tips?**

A   *At the very least, always use a pen and paper, so that you can jot down the
letters in different orders for experimenting. You may find it even easier to
tear off separate pieces for each letter so you can physically shuffle them
around.*

Q   What types of information lend themselves best to acronyms?

A   *Long names, lists and any collections of words. Although they are usually
used for technical and scientific information (e.g. lists of bones or nerves in
medicine), they can equally be used to memorise a number of points that
you wish to be able to regurgitate in, for instance, a speech or exam. They
can be a little like a checklist. In that instance, each major point will need
to be represented by a single word which will trigger that whole point
easily.*

44

How to remember a country's capital

Become a walking atlas!

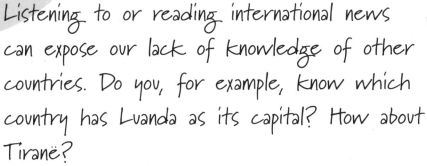

Listening to or reading international news can expose our lack of knowledge of other countries. Do you, for example, know which country has Luanda as its capital? How about Tiranë?

While most of us will only need to memorise the capitals of countries for geography exams at school, it can still be a useful thing to know. For example, when you meet someone from a less well-known country, they may be impressed if you already know the capital of their nation. Equally, knowing a nation's capital, and something about it (such as a landmark), will help you to remember more information about it in the future as it gives you something to connect and associate it with.

Visualising the capital's landmark is really the key to burning it into your memory. Think London and you immediately think of Big Ben; Paris, the Eiffel Tower. If you see those images, you immediately think of those cities. Use an atlas, travel book or the Internet to find one memorable image, such as a similar landmark, for each

Rather than memorising a long list of capital cities, try memorising as much information as you can about the capital city of a country you intend to visit in the near future. The more facts you can remember about it, the easier you will find it to learn more.

capital city. Having a single visual image for each city will make it far easier to bring to mind.

Beware, however, of red-herring landmark images. For example, when thinking of a landmark that represents America, the Statue of Liberty (in New York) might come to mind for some before the White House or the Lincoln Memorial (which are both in Washington DC). Equally, when thinking of Australia, people often immediately picture the Sydney Opera House or the harbour bridge. Images of landmarks in Australia's capital, Canberra, are not so widely known. This only underlines the importance of researching an image for each capital if you can't already recall one. If you can vividly imagine an image of Canberra, it makes it far less likely that you'll fall into the trap of picturing the Sydney Opera House whenever you try to recall the capital of Australia.

You then need to create a mental image which ties the country to the name of its capital and, ideally, the image of its prime landmark. Firstly, start by taking the very first association that comes to mind when you think of a particular country. This is important, as the first association is likely to be the most memorable thing in the future too. With countries that you are less familiar with, this becomes easier. For example, I associate my home country, England, with many things, but I don't know much about Uruguay. The first thing that comes to mind when I think of that country is football. Their capital is Montevideo, which makes me think of people watching a video of the 60s TV comedy show *Monty Python* (Monty sounds like Monte). Finally, a quick search online shows that a prominent landmark of

Montevideo is a large plaza, called the Plaza Independencia. So, the image I would use to remember this all is of a group of footballers, taking a break from playing a game in the plaza to sit and watch a TV outside (this makes the image more incongruous and hence memorable), then a giant cartoon foot comes down from the sky and squashes them (reminiscent of the *Monty Python* show).

Like all great travellers, I have seen more than I remember, and remember more than I have seen.
BENJAMIN DISRAELI

Defining idea...

Now, have a go at making your own connections with the following countries, all beginning with 'A'. If you don't know anything about a country, just take a guess: the first thing that comes into your mind about that country.

Country	Capital	Landmark	Mental image
Afghanistan	Kabul	The snow-topped Hindu Kush mountains	
Albania	Tiranë	Et'hem Bey Mosque	
Algeria	Algiers	Harbour	
Andorra	Andorra la Vella	Valley	
Angola	Luanda	Fortress of São Miguel	
Antigua	St John's	Cathedral	
Argentina	Buenos Aires	The Obelisk	
Australia	Canberra	Parliament House building	
Austria	Vienna	Amusement fair with ferris wheel	

The easiest way to make a mental image for the capital is to think about what it sounds like. For example, Kabul, the capital of Afghanistan, sounds to me like cable, and makes me think of a cable car. This fits perfectly with the landmark of Kabul: I imagine a cable car going up the Hindu Kush mountains.

How did it go?

Q I'd like to learn every country in the world, but it's a daunting task. Any tips?

A *Just try and learn one a day. If you are learning a large number of capitals, you may also like to use a world map, so you can see where each country is.*

Q Are there any general patterns that can be used to remember capitals?

A *Some countries have what I call a twin capital city, which is where the name of their capital city is the same as that of the country. Examples of this include Andorra (Andorra la Vella), Kuwait (Kuwait City), Mexico (Mexico City), Guatemala (Guatemala City) and Singapore. In these cases, you could represent this fact that the name is repeated by creating a mental image of its landmark, with a reflection in water (so there are two of it).*

45

Dream memory projects

We spend about a third of our lives asleep, but it's a time when a memory is shut out.

We don't remember most of our dreams, and when we are dreaming we don't remember we're in bed! Breaking through this barrier can achieve some amazing results.

We spend many thousands of hours each year dreaming, yet it all occurs under a veil of forgetting. It's a curious thing that there is a barrier in our conscious awareness between our waking mind and our sleeping mind.

The key to keeping hold of your memories for the night's dreams is to make this your first thought when you wake up: what have I been dreaming? Do this before you open your eyes, or even before you move. As soon as you start moving around and focusing on the outside world, your memories of your dreams will begin to fade. Many people find that bringing their dreams into conscious awareness gives them both a source of creative ideas and an insight into their own minds.

However, as well as bringing your dreams into consciousness, you can also bring your consciousness into dreams. Lucid dreaming is where you are having a dream, and you suddenly remember that it's a dream. Because you have become conscious

Try keeping a dream diary in order to get into the habit of remembering your dreams. Simply keep a notebook and pencil next to your bed, and when you wake up in the morning – or even in the middle of the night – and can remember what you had been dreaming about, jot down as many details as possible. All new memories quickly fade away if we don't think about them, and particularly memories of our dreams. This means you should jot down your dreams quickly as soon as you wake.

of this, you are able to take control of the dream and experience anything you like, as though it were really happening. I'm sure you can see the appeal of lucid dreaming!

While there is an awful lot to be said on the subject of lucid dreaming, there are basically just four main techniques that you need to know about in order to give yourself the best chances of experiencing it.

Have a strong motivation to experience lucid dreaming

I'll be honest with you: lucid dreaming is not easy to learn for most people, and there are no short cuts. It may take some time and a lot of effort to reach the point where you can regularly experience lucid dreams. So if you are interested in learning to lucid dream, I would strongly suggest not wasting any time searching for short cuts, and instead get to work on practising the next techniques. But in order to give yourself the enthusiasm and stamina needed to persist long enough to master the technique, think about all the amazing and useful things you could do if you could lucid dream at will. For example, think of the levels of freedom you could experience...

Get into the habit of asking 'is this a dream?'

Next, get yourself into the habit of asking yourself at regular points during the day 'is this a dream?' If your mind gets into this habit

Who looks outside, dreams.
Who looks inside, awakens.
CARL JUNG

Defining idea...

during the day, there is a greater chance of you asking yourself that question while you are asleep. One way to do this is to ask yourself the question at the beginning of each hour throughout the day. You could even set the alarm on your watch or mobile phone to go off at regular intervals to remind you to do so.

Hold in mind the strong intention to lucid dream as you go to sleep

As you lie in bed before going to sleep, concentrate your mind on the idea that you will have a lucid dream. Some people also suggest trying to keep your mind awake while your body goes to sleep by concentrating on one thought or idea, or by just deliberately telling yourself that you will remain conscious. Try and do this every night before you drift off to sleep.

Try waking up, then going back to sleep

Finally, try waking yourself up early in the morning, then going back to sleep (again, as you drift off to sleep, concentrate on the idea that you will have a lucid dream). People are most likely to experience lucid dreams in the hours just before they would usually awaken in the morning; by waking up a bit earlier, and then going back to sleep, you are most likely to improve your chances of experiencing a lucid dream.

How did it go?

Q **I tried the lucid dream techniques and they didn't work. What should I do?**

A *You just need to persist; this is not an easy technique. But follow the instructions and sooner or later you will experience a lucid dream.*

Q **I experienced a lucid dream, but it was a bit fuzzy and indistinct, then I woke up within a minute. Where am I going wrong?**

A *It's also worth mentioning that not all lucid dreams (or ordinary dreams for that matter) are of equal quality. Some will be hyper-realistic, in fact can be more realistic than everyday life (for example, the clarity and vividness of your vision in such a lucid dream can be better than in your waking life). However, some dreams are of lesser quality; they look more vague, and maybe are even kind of black and white or 'washed out' rather than in vivid colour. Equally, in some lucid dreams you can gain an amazing amount of control, willing yourself to meet certain people, travel to certain places and basically experience anything you want to – yet in other lucid dreams you may struggle to control events. Your control of what is happening may be more clumsy, and after a while may slip away completely; you drift back into the ordinary dream state, forgetting that you are dreaming. I only mention these points so that you will not feel disappointed if your lucid dreams are not spectacular to begin with. They can be, so keep going until you experience one!*

46

Remember your reading

Ever read a page, or even a chapter, then realised you can't remember any of it?

Here's how to boost your memory for books.

It's been estimated that up to three quarters of what we know was gleaned through reading. Yet we rarely put effort into improving our ability to retain what we learn from reading. By making a greater effort to concentrate and understand your reading you will remember more of it. Here are some tips for improving your learning from non-fiction reading.

Know your goal
Before you begin reading a book or article, be clear on what you wish to learn from it. This will help focus your attention as you read to pick out the most important bits, and hence help you remember them. Write out a list of questions that you hope to find the answers to and, as you do, jot them down.

Get an overview first
Before you start a book, first gain an overview of it by looking at the contents, cover description and skimming through it. See if you can get a sense of its structure and main themes. You may also like to read reviews of the book online. This preparation will help you to understand the material when you are reading the book properly. Greater understanding equals stronger memory retention.

Here's an idea for you...

Reading fiction is usually more of an entertainment, and remembering facts from a novel is not so important. Nevertheless, memory can help your enjoyment of a novel: each time a new character appears, pause and try to create a visual image of them based upon the author's description.

Don't read like a zombie

Don't try and read while doing other things. If you are listening to the radio, holding a conversation or even thinking about something else while you are trying to read, your attention is divided and therefore weakened. Indeed, this often results in what I call 'zombie' reading, where your eyes are moving across the words, but you are not paying any conscious attention to what you're actually reading. If you ever find you've read a page or more but have no memory of what you've only just read, then you've been zombie reading! Go back and re-read that section. If you find your thoughts are repeatedly straying onto other things, it may be time to take a break. You can also avoid this by reading in limited bursts of no more than an hour at a time.

Create your own index

The index of a book helps the reader to find important concepts within the book. However, a powerful memory technique is to construct your own, personalised index for each non-fiction book you read. This will not only make it far easier for you to find information in the future, but will act as a superb memory prompt. Along with your chapter summaries, just skimming through this information will help you recall the main points of the book.

Mark the book in pencil

As you are reading, it's very useful to have a pencil in your hand. For one thing, reading with a pencil helps to direct and focus your attention by directing your eye movements. Another benefit is that you can underline or otherwise mark key points (I use a five-star system: a mildly important point will get one asterisk next to it, all the way up to five for an extremely valuable point). Also, you can even jot down your own thoughts in the margins.

Focus your attention on the beginnings and ends

Typically, the beginnings and ends of each section – of the book, of each chapter, and even of each paragraph – are usually the most 'content rich'. The same is true of articles. If you just want to extract the main points of an article, without spending the time to read the whole thing, you can usually do so by just reading the first and last paragraphs.

Create chapter summaries

As you finish each chapter, write a short (one paragraph) summary of its key points. If you find that you can't, and that you didn't understand what the chapter was trying to say, then go back and read it again. Writing chapter summaries not only keeps your attention focused while you're reading, but acts as a perfect aide-memoire when you are thinking back to the contents of the book months or years later.

Defining idea...

Reading helps to stimulate the transition between short-term memory to long-term memory by exercising the ability to understand events that happened earlier and later in a book.

DR WON JANG-WON, dementia researcher

How did it go?

Q   I really don't like to write in a book. Is this essential?

A   Many people have an aversion to writing in books. They feel that this will despoil or even ruin the book. However, I'd ask you to rethink this. Firstly, if you use a pencil, and write relatively lightly, then it needn't mark the book permanently: you can always erase the marks in the future. Secondly, it can actually make a book more interesting to find previously written comments or underlinings in it: whether these were written by yourself or someone else.

Q   Will remembering more of what I read help my memory in general?

A   Studies with elderly people show that regular reading can be beneficial in keeping their memories sharp. Also, the more you remember what you've read, the more knowledge you will retain, and therefore you'll have more memories to associate new facts with.

Q   I've heard that speaking out words in your mind while you are reading is bad and you should try to eliminate it. Is this right?

A   There's no good evidence that this is true.

47

Use your memory to become a genius (it only takes ten years)!

New research shows that geniuses are not just born, often they are made – and the key is that they build up a vast memory bank of info in their particular field.

Believing you need to be born with special talents might be stopping you from achieving your true potential.

Could it be that genius-level performance is actually due to constructing a large databank of memory info in your chosen field? We think of geniuses as being born special, but the latest research shows that they are more likely to be the product of hard work. Many star thinkers are not actually mentally calculating or computing the answers to problems so much as tapping into vast memory stores they've built up through years of study and practice. Where a beginner or average performer has to work things out step by step, the genius simply pulls out pre-formed solutions from memory, or manipulates large 'chunks' of memory at once. These usually pop into consciousness without them even having to think too hard!

A good example of this is chess. A lot of evidence on genius performance comes from studies on chess grandmasters as it's an easily measured skill. Chess players are

Here's an idea for you...

Think of an area you are skilled in that you would like to progress far further in. Make a list of problems in that field that you're uncertain of being able to crack, and resolve to solve them! Join organisations and groups in that field for whom you only just qualify. Spend time with people who are slightly more skilled than you in the area you are trying to master.

basically genius-researchers' ideal lab rats. Here's what's been discovered. Grandmasters have an extremely good memory for chess positions, although their memory in general is no better than that of weak players (nor do they have any other special, inborn skills like superior spatial abilities). In other words, they have trained themselves to have a very specific, highly structured body of memories for chess positions. They don't even have to consider the positions of each piece individually; they can see whole patterns of pieces together in one go. In essence, their experience gives them a map which they can quickly scan to find the best 'route' in any particular situation. When solving a chess problem, the weaker players are like a person standing in a maze, having to physically walk step by step through different directions in order to discover the best route. But the grandmasters are like a person with a map of the maze: one glance and they can see the best route.

These memory maps are, obviously, built up through experience; we're not born with them. For example, a Hungarian psychologist, Làszló Polgàr, set out to prove that geniuses are made by using his own daughters as guinea pigs. From a young age, Polgàr put his three home-schooled daughters through a rigorous daily programme of chess playing and studying. Eventually, one went on to become the world's first female grandmaster, another also became a grandmaster and the third became an international master.

Evidence shows that the same process of building up rich memory maps occurs in other fields too, such as music, computer programming and playing bridge. Young star performers in any field may appear to have been born gifted, but have probably just started early and worked hard at their speciality. Leopold Mozart, like Làszló Polgàr, began teaching his son, Wolfgang Amadeus, music at the age of four, and he went on to become one of the greatest musical geniuses of all time.

Nothing in the world can take the place of persistence... Persistence and determination alone are omnipotent.
CALVIN COOLIDGE

Defining idea...

The key is that you must engage in continuous, effortful practice and study: you've got to keep stretching yourself. The typical person who regularly practises a skill, like playing golf, tends to quickly plateau out at a moderate level. They don't constantly try for higher levels of competitive performance.

Another key is high levels of motivation: you can't force yourself to become a genius in something you're not somewhat obsessed with. If you are fascinated by something and driven to master it, then the long hours of practice will come naturally.

While this research doesn't prove that there's no such thing as an inborn special 'spark' of talent in some people, it does show how easily we've underestimated hard work. In fact, too strong a belief in innate talent can be detrimental, even to someone regarded as talented. For example, if a child believes that they are talented, then that also means that they believe things should come easier to them, which can count against them putting in long hours of effortful practice. It can also mean that they get discouraged easily when they encounter setbacks (they can start to doubt their talent, and then avoid future competition in order to shelter themselves from having to face any more uncomfortable failures). It's far better for a child (or adult!) to see themselves as hard working, as the research shows this is the real key to high performance.

How did it go?

Q   **I don't have ten years to become a genius, isn't there a quicker route?**

A   *Unfortunately there is no short cut to such high levels of performance. However, you could accelerate your journey to genius by more intensive practice. The more hours per week you put in, the sooner you'll get there. Also, make sure that your practice is continually challenging you to improve.*

Q   **I have a young son, does this research mean I have an obligation to train him to become a genius?**

A   *Pushing a young child hard in an area in which they haven't shown a natural interest could be seen as unhealthy. But if your child is enthusiastic about something, then it could hugely aid his development to help him onto a programme of challenging practice. Whatever your son's interests, though, it is good to teach him the value of working hard to master things, rather than expecting all high performance to come from inborn talent.*

48

Learn foreign menus

It's the place you're most likely to have to deal with foreign languages. Here's how to learn the names of the most common dishes in unfamiliar tongues.

Have you ever experienced the feeling of dread upon opening a restaurant's menu, only to realise that it's entirely in a language you don't understand?

Perhaps you avoid native restaurants when travelling, simply due to the fear of being unable to comprehend the menu? Instead, you confine your eating to one of the international fast-food joints where every menu is the same. Safe and maybe even comforting, but it prevents you from experiencing the full variety of the local culture. Eating out in a foreign country, or even in a restaurant in your home city which serves foreign cuisine, can be one of the times when your lack of knowledge of another language can be most frustrating.

There are several things you can do to prepare for eating out in a foreign country before you even set foot there. Firstly, you could visit a restaurant serving that country's cuisine in your own home city. They are probably more likely to have each dish's description in English too, and to have a waiter who is far more used to providing explanations. This will allow you to prepare in relative safety, without the

Here's an idea for you...

Each time you try a foreign cuisine, try a different dish. This will give you a greater number of memory 'hooks' to associate with the names of various dishes, making it more likely that you will recognise them in the future when you are scanning through a foreign menu. Keep a diary of the different foreign meals you've tried, recording what they tasted like, and how much you liked them.

more embarrassing situation of having to ask a waiter abroad for explanations in English, which he may or may not be able to provide.

Secondly, spend some time learning the words for your favourite dishes, or favourite foods and/or ingredients. That way you'll at least be able to get a general feel for whether you'll like a dish, even if you only recognise one of the words in its description. Lastly, and perhaps most importantly, learn the words for any dishes, foods or ingredients you wish to avoid, either because you hate them or are allergic to them. If you do happen to be allergic to something, you may also like to memorise the phrase 'Does this dish contain...?' so you can ask the waiter.

Also, the perennially powerful technique of using mental imagery can help you memorise particular words for food. Here are a couple of examples:

- The French for fish is poisson. This is similar to *poison*. So you could imagine a man choking on a poisonous fish (not that I want to put you off ordering it!).
- The Spanish for chicken is *pollo*. To remember this, you could envisage a cartoon chicken playing polo on horseback.

There are some other things you can do.

Use your cellphone camera
If you are staying some time in a foreign country, take a tour around the local restaurants and locate those which post their menus outside. Study them and jot

down any of the dishes you can't understand. You could also, if you have one, take a photo or two of the menu with your mobile phone camera. This will give you a lot of information that you can then look up in your own time. You can also do this when sitting with your menu in a restaurant, although it might be best to be discreet about it.

The only cooks in the civilized world are French cooks... Other nations understand food in general; the French alone understand cooking.
LOUIS VICTOR NESTOR ROCOPLAN, French journalist and theatre administrator

Defining idea...

Take a guess

Many foreign words are similar to their English equivalent. For example, even if you don't speak German, I'm sure you can guess what the word *fisch* means, or the French word *brocoli*. If you guess at the meaning of particular words within the dish's description, you can often work out what the course is.

Memorise the sections

Another way to focus your memorising time and effort would be to memorise the words for each major section, such as 'appetisers', 'main courses' and 'deserts'. This would then at least give you a little more confidence in navigating any menu in that language.

Create a cheat sheet

If you don't have time to memorise all the words you need, you could always jot them down on a piece of paper, or store them on your phone and discreetly glance at it in the restaurant. This may seem counter-productive as you are trying to boost your memory skills, but the very act of doing this will contribute to the learning process.

How did it go?

Q **Don't most menus already have an English translation for each item?**

A   *Some do. But it's mostly those restaurants in the more tourist-centric areas. If you truly want to experience the authentic restaurants in a country, the chances are likely that they'll be in the foreign format.*

Q **What about pronunciation?**

A   *Just being able to recognise the meaning of a dish's description is clearly better than not being able to. It will enable you to make an informed choice about your order. You'll be able to locate the things you like and avoid the things you hate. However, as you correctly point out, pronunciation is important. For this you'll need to check. You can either spend the time preparing when you memorise, or you can take a guess as you declare your choice to the waiter. If you make eye contact with him and speak clearly, there's a good chance he'll understand you, even if your pronunciation isn't perfect.*

49

How to find lost items

It's one of the most annoying lapses of memory: where did I leave my...?

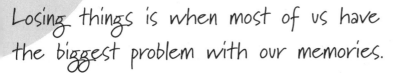
Losing things is when most of us have the biggest problem with our memories.

These lapses can range from the merely annoying (where did I leave the TV remote control?) to the panic-inducing ones (losing your passport on the night before your holiday).

If you regularly lose things, don't necessarily assume you have a bad memory. It's probably more likely that you are disorganised. If your home or work environment is cluttered, messy and chaotic, it's going to make it harder for you to recall the position of things. Keeping things tidy and in order and avoiding clutter can be a good prevention against losing items. Alternatively, you're more likely to lose things when you have a lot on your mind, and your attention is consumed with other matters: the 'absent-minded professor syndrome'. If you are prone to forgetting where you left things due to thinking about other things, it's probably no use to simply tell you to 'pay more attention'; you already know you should! Just get yourself into the habit of keeping important items in sight, or in a regular place.

Help your memory by having fixed storage places for valuable items. Things that you take with you each time you go out (such as wallet/purse, keys, etc.) can be stored together, perhaps near the front door, so they are easy to retrieve and leave when you go in and out. A little bit of organisation can save a lot of anxious energy later if things get lost!

However, if you do lose something, I recommend that you implement this four-stage emergency plan.

Stage one: don't panic!

Losing something can put anyone into a panicked state of mind. This is often counter-productive and can impede you finding the item. In order to visually scan your environment for the item, you are going to need a clear head to pay attention; panic is going to work against you. So, first take a moment to calm yourself. Take some slow, deep breaths and sit down. Do not start your search until you are perfectly calm. If you can afford to, try taking your mind off the problem for a while. Sometimes, simply by relaxing, you may realise where you left the item.

Stage two: work out the last known location

Where did you last use or see the item? Or, if it wasn't you, who was the last person to use or see it? Spend a couple of minutes to think carefully about this as it's the single biggest clue you have to its location. Most objects end up being within inches of where you last saw them or where they 'should' be. Is it very near to where it should be, but fallen into, behind or underneath something? Could someone have borrowed or moved the item?

Stage three: plan your search – narrow down the possible locations

If you have answered the last question, then you should have already narrowed down the range of possible locations to search. Simply searching everywhere – for example, in every room of your house – is inefficient. You need to first work out a shortlist of which rooms this item could possibly be in and then, out of those, which it is most likely to be in. Then you need to work out which areas within those rooms it is most likely to be in. Think about where you might have been using the item. Also think about the shape and size of the item, as this will determine where it could be. Something flat, like a credit card, piece of paper or book, could be easily hidden within a pile of papers, whereas a larger item couldn't. What 'hiding places' – drawers, bags, pockets – are the right size to accommodate your item?

Stage four: search carefully and systematically

People waste a lot of time looking for objects by going over and over the same areas. It's quite common, when in a panic, to actually look straight at the object and not register that you've found it, and just continue looking, because the panic is stopping you from paying clear attention. Resolve to only look in each area once. This means you will need to take a slower, thorough and more methodical approach, but ultimately it will save you time.

Praising what is lost makes the remembrance dear.
WILLIAM SHAKESPEARE

Defining idea...

How did it go?

Q   I often lose computer files. How can I remember where they are?

A   *With many of us using more than one computer, and having a range of storage media (DVDs, USB memory sticks, etc.) it can be hard to keep track of our digital information. Aside from keeping your discs and external storage media organised and together in order, the best thing you can do is always name each file with a clear description. That way, even if lost, you stand a chance of finding it through your computer's search facilities.*

Q   I often see the object I'm looking for but, in my searching frenzy, look straight through it without recognising it. How can I avoid this?

A   *As you are searching, talk to yourself, describing each thing you pick up or search through. This will keep your attention focused and ensure that you don't fail to recognise the item when you do find it.*

Q   I do try to narrow down my searches by asking myself 'where is it most likely to be', but sometimes the lost item isn't in the room where I thought it would be. Isn't this technique useless?

A   *No, you've merely made a mistake in your assumptions of where it could be. Think back more carefully of all the places you could have had the object or, if you lost it recently, recall the rooms you were last in. Alternatively, rather than think of which rooms it's most likely to be in, try to eliminate those it is impossible for it to be in.*

50

Create an historical peg system

How to remember history.

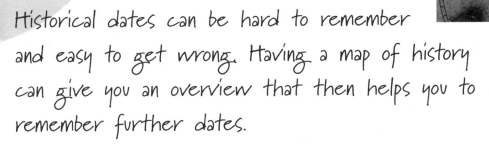

Historical dates can be hard to remember and easy to get wrong. Having a map of history can give you an overview that then helps you to remember further dates.

You can often work out the approximate dates by developing a sequence of events. For example, imagine you are trying to remember the date when the Japanese bombed Pearl Harbor. You may not be able to recall the date, but you do know that it occurred during World War Two, which ran from 1939 to 1945, so it must be within that time frame. You also know that the Americans didn't fight during the first couple of years (which eliminates 1939 and 1940) of the war, and because they *did* fight for about three years, this eliminates at least 1943, 1944 and 1945. That narrows the event down to between 1941 and 1942 (and it actually occurred in December 1941). Of course, this technique only works if you already know something about the historical period you are trying to remember. It therefore helps to first get an overview of history; to understand, even basically, the human story.

Here's an idea for you...

Create and memorise a map of your own past. Although you are unlikely to ever sit an examination testing you on which year various events occurred in your life, it can be enormously helpful to remember what you did each year. Get a notebook and write down each year of your life so far. Then, next to each year, try to write several key events. The more time you spend on this, the more likely you will continue to remember more and more events you thought were long forgotten.

An historical peg system is a rough outline of a period of history that you can memorise in order to know the context of events. If you already have this skeleton structure, it makes it far easier to learn future dates. Remember, memories are like money: the more you have, the easier it is to get more! Like a jigsaw puzzle, even just putting in a number of key pieces helps you to begin to see the overall shape of the picture, and then helps you slot in more pieces.

There are two main ways to create an historical peg system. Firstly, you can concentrate on remembering a small number of dates. The best way to do this is to make up a little rhyme for each year. For example, 509 BC – the Romans raised a glass of wine, when they became a republic in 5-0-9.

If you make up a memorable rhyme for each period of 500 years (i.e. 1000 BC, 500 BC, 0, AD 500, AD 1000, AD 1500), for example, you can create a map of long periods of history. Alternatively, if you wanted to create an even larger time line of history, you could use an exponential sequence of dates, such as 10, 100, 1000 and 10,000 years ago.

You can adapt this particular peg system to meet your own interests and needs. For instance, my examples are particularly focused on Western history. You may be more interested, perhaps, in the long history of Chinese civilisation or you may not be interested in general historical events so much as scientific and technical discoveries. In that case you could create a peg system to reflect this, with, perhaps a greater density of pegs in the recent past as the pace of invention accelerated. You may find it preferable to memorise the years of rule of various kings, queens or heads of state.

History is just one damn thing after another.
ANON

Defining idea...

The second method is to turn history into a story, and then plant dates into the story at key points. As an example, I'll take the history of the industrial revolution. We'll begin in 1776 with the invention of the steam engine by James Watt. Visualise a giant steam engine with the number 1776 embossed on its front, its pistons and wheels moving and steam pouring forth from it. Then imagine that there are ten of these, and the tenth one is powering a cotton mill (visualise the big reels of cotton). This represents the fact that it was ten years after its invention that the steam engine was used in cotton mills. Then, outside the cotton mill, imagine a Victorian man standing at a train platform, impatiently consulting his pocket watch, which says 18:01; the train is one minute late! This represents the fact that the first steam train was demonstrated in 1801. Finally, imagine Morse tapping away in the railway station on his telegraph system, sending a morse code faster to the next station than either a bird or a boomerang flying through the air. This represents the fact that Morse invented the telegraph system in 1837 (the number 3 can look like a flying bird – turn your head to the right! – and 7 can look like a boomerang). This is an extremely simplified example, but it's just to give you an idea of the principle.

221

How did
it go?

Q **Sometimes even the historians can't agree on a particular date. What should I do when there's more than one date in use?**

A   *It's very rare that you will ever need to know a precise date in such circumstances. If there's more than one accepted date, then you should be fine just remembering one of them. Typically, especially for ancient history, an approximate date will usually suffice.*

Q **Can I use any other memory techniques to learn historical dates?**

A   *Yes. Of particular use are techniques for turning numbers into letters. However, the techniques of imagery and stories used here can be adequate in most cases. The more vividly you can imagine an historical event, the more memorable it becomes. Seek out movies set in the periods of history you're trying to learn about (but make sure they're as accurate as possible).*

51

Memory party tricks

How to win friends and influence people with your new-found memory powers.

Most people are interested in how to improve their memories in everyday life, how to learn to remember names, perhaps. But if you just want to show off this is the idea for you!

How to remember jokes

There's a story – possibly apocryphal – about a group of bored soldiers who wanted a faster way to tell each other their favourite jokes. Rather than recite each joke in full, they memorised a number for each one, so that any of them would merely have to shout 'five!' or 'twelve!' and they would all collapse in hysterical laughter.

While you could memorise a batch of jokes that way, you would still be wise to recite the actual joke rather than the number at a party! The great thing about jokes is that they come with features that already make them easy to memorise. Humour inherently makes information easier to remember, as does the silly or larger-than-life nature of many jokes. This makes the structure of the joke itself relatively easy to remember, although you may still want to practise a few times. Through doing this you will learn the best way of telling the joke, and avoid saying things like 'oh,

Even if you don't want to show off your memory at a party, it can be a great opportunity to practise remembering names. At the end of the party – assuming you aren't drunk – try and recall the names of all the new people you met. Then try and recall them again the following morning. Remember, the best way to burn a name into your memory is to repeat it upon meeting the person, and try and build an association between their name and the way they look.

hang on, I need to remember how it goes' which tends to ruin the punchline.

Like the bored soldiers, you can create a memorised list of jokes by associating each with a number. Using the number-shape method, you could link each joke to a visual image of something that looks like each number (e.g. a swan for two, handcuffs for three, and so on). Using this method you can easily remember a list of ten jokes.

How to memorise a pack of cards

Do you think it's impossible to memorise a pack of cards, in order, looking only once at each card? It's not. In 2002, Dominic O'Brien did just this and, because he wanted to make it a little more of a challenge, he added an extra fifty-three packs, had them all shuffled together randomly, and spent the next twelve hours memorising them successfully in order. That's 2808 cards. OK, so Dominic is the eight-times world memory champion, and this little feat *did* win him a Guinness world record. Nevertheless, memorising just one pack doesn't seem so hard now, does it?

The key to memorising a pack of cards is to turn each card into a person. For example, the queen of diamonds might be Shirley Bassey, the singer famous for 'Diamonds are Forever'. The jack of clubs might be Jack Nicklaus (the famous golfer, hence the link to clubs). The number cards are a little trickier, and you'll need to get creative to make associative links for them. You can link the number to something you already associate with it (the ten of clubs might be Dudley Moore, who starred in the film *10*, playing the piano in a nightclub), or link it to something which looks or sounds like it (so the seven of spades might be an Australian farmer leaning on a spade – the figure 7 looks like a boomerang).

> *It's a strange sort of memory that only works backwards!*
> LEWIS CARROLL – the Queen in *Alice in Wonderland*.

Defining idea...

Each character should be one that you can instantly bring to mind when you see that card, so you'll need to spend some time preparing. The character should then also have an action (like Shirley Bassey singing). Finally, you need a journey, in order to memorise the list of cards in order. This could be your route to work (as long as there are a selection of easily visualised landmarks along the way, or a route around your home). You'll need twenty-six points along this journey, so unless you have a large house, you'll need two or three areas in each room where you can mentally place each character.

Then, to put it all together, you will remember cards in pairs. Starting with the first card, you imagine the person who represents that card, doing the action of the person of the next card, then place that person at the first point in your journey.

Recite a memorised list forwards and backwards

At a party, or in a group of people, you can get them to challenge you to memorise a long list of items. By using the journey method, you can mentally associate each item with a stage on your journey. Just make sure you have mentally prepared the journey beforehand, and know the order of your route. When using the journey method to memorise a list, it's just as easy to recite the items backwards as it is forwards. All you need to do is mentally traverse your journey in the opposite direction, beginning with the last item. Yet there's something that always impresses people when you recite the list backwards.

How did it go?

Q   Any other memory tricks that I can use in social situations?

A   *Using the same technique that I suggested for remembering jokes, you could remember ten interesting facts – perhaps sporting statistics if your friends are sports fans.*

Q   Are there any practical benefits with learning to memorise a deck of cards, or is it purely a fancy trick?

A   *It won't necessarily improve your memory in general, but it will almost certainly boost your powers of concentration.*

Q   Any tips for making reciting a list backwards more impressive?

A   *A good memory trick, like a good magic trick, requires a bit of play-acting and drama to make it truly impressive. Pretend to struggle as you recite the list forwards, making it seem difficult. Then recite it backwards quickly to achieve a suitably impressive effect!*

How to pass exams

Good memory strategies can revolutionise your exam performance.

Got exams coming up? Don't panic! By following a few key memory tips you can avert the nightmare of forgetfulness and boost your performance.

No other events in our lives put so much demand on our memories to perform well as exams. Once you are in an exam, all you have is your memory. There are no opportunities to go and look information up in a book or online. As if this wasn't bad enough, the clock is always ticking: you have to remember things quickly!

Start your revision as early as possible, giving you enough time to make sure you understand all the material, and so you can pace yourself well. When revising, do so without any distractions. Dividing your attention between your revision and the TV or radio will diminish your ability to encode the information in your long-term memory. Ration your exposure to entertainments, and instead use them as rewards for completing your revision goals.

Get as much practice as you can in answering questions from previous exams, under exam conditions. Give yourself the same time limit that you'd have in the actual exam,

Here's an idea for you...

Make a revision timetable that takes into account the best time schedule for reviewing information, so that it gets a better chance of being burned into your long-term memory. Don't just plan when you are going to study each topic area, but add when you will need to review that topic: one day, one week, and (if you have time), one month later. Also plan to end each revision session with a quick review of the material you've just covered.

and answer the paper in silence and without breaks. Practising under the same conditions as you will face in the real exam is more beneficial than under unnatural conditions. Equally, try to match the same, or similar conditions when you are revising. We recall information better if we are in similar environmental conditions to those we learned it in.

Use plenty of regular self-tests when revising as well as practising with past papers. Take ten-minute breaks between revision sessions, and then test yourself on the material you've just learned. This gives you the best chance at retaining the information. Use these tests to identify your weakest areas, so that you can put in extra work on revising those. Which bits of information do you find it hardest to recall? Do you understand those areas fully? Just putting the information in front of your eyes repeatedly is not enough to improve your memory for it. You must actually think about the information.

Don't try to study through the night or when you are overly tired, even if you do drink coffee or cola to perk yourself up. You may feel confident that you can revise like that, but research shows that, despite no drop in confidence, tired people are not good at revising.

Learn the material as deeply as you can. While repetition has its place within your arsenal of memory techniques (and it *will* be important to you in revising for exams), it's far better to first understand the material deeply. Not only will you be in a better position to analyse and interpret the information in your exam questions, but you'll also be more likely to remember it.

An investment in knowledge always pays the best interest.
BENJAMIN FRANKLIN

Defining idea...

While understanding is important for all revision, different learning techniques will be required for different types of exam, so let's look at those.

- For mathematical questions (such as in maths, physics, chemistry and computer science): practise and, if you need to, memorise key equations and laws.
- For essay-based questions: practise writing essays at speed. Memorise key facts, lists and quotes. Spend the first few minutes of the exam making notes for how you intend to answer the essay. Many essays ask you to compare and contrast, or discuss different views. Prepare for this by having discussions about main subject areas with your fellow students.
- For short answer questions: memorise key facts, lists and quotes. Try explaining facts to a friend or family member to ensure that you understand them well and are able to articulate them.

In the hours before your exam, try to relax as much as you can. A relaxed and clear state of mind is best for recall. Make sure you eat a good breakfast and keep your blood sugar up before you enter the exam. In the exam itself, spend several minutes reading through the paper before you begin to answer any questions. With a pencil, make a note of any questions that you can't immediately recall the answers to. If you take note of these at the beginning of the exam, your unconscious mind may have time to recall the answers by the end.

And, once the exams are over – relax. You can afford to forget all that information now, and your real education can begin!

231

How did it go?

Q How do I know which subjects to revise first?

A *Begin with those areas which you don't yet fully understand. This will give you as much time as possible to understand and remember them. Next, move on to those areas which you do understand, but find hardest to remember. This will give you plenty of time to repeat and review the information in your mind.*

Q What should I do if my memory fails me in the exam?

A *First, relax. Panicking will only make it harder to remember. Jot down any ideas which come to mind. This should help to shake loose any hard-to-remember bits of information. Try to think back to when you were revising the information. Recalling the environment you were in when you were studying will help you to recall the information. If you can't remember the information fully, write down whatever you can remember, as you may still be awarded marks for that.*

The end...

Or is it a new beginning?

We hope that these ideas will have shown you plenty of new ways to improve your powers of recall. We hope you've found some interesting tips and techniques that will make easier to remember people's names, all the facts you need for the big exam or what it was, precisely, that you went upstairs to find. You can never expect to remember *everything* but hopefully you've started to notice a continual improvement in your memory.

So why not let us know about it? Tell us how you got on. What did it for you – which ideas really helped to hone your mind? Maybe you've got some tips of your own that you'd like to share. And if you liked this book you may find we have even more brilliant ideas that could help change other areas of your life for the better.

You'll find the Infinite Ideas crew waiting for you online at www.infideas.com.

Or if you prefer to write, then send your letters to:
Boost your memory
Infinite Ideas Ltd
36 St Giles, Oxford, OX1 3LD, United Kingdom

We want to know what you think, because we're all working on making our lives better too. Give us your feedback and you could win a copy of another **52 Brilliant Ideas** book of your choice. Or maybe get a crack at writing your own.

Good luck. Be brilliant.

Offer one

CASH IN YOUR IDEAS

We hope you enjoy this book. We hope it inspires, amuses, educates and entertains you. But we don't assume that you're a novice, or that this is the first book that you've bought on the subject. You've got ideas of your own. Maybe our author has missed an idea that you use successfully. If so, why not send it to yourauthormissedatrick@infideas.com, and if we like it we'll post it on our bulletin board. Better still, if your idea makes it into print we'll send you four books of your choice or the cash equivalent. You'll be fully credited so that everyone knows you've had another Brilliant Idea.

Offer two

HOW COULD YOU REFUSE?

Amazing discounts on bulk quantities of Infinite Ideas books are available to corporations, professional associations and other organisations.

For details call us on:
+44 (0)1865 514888
Fax: +44 (0)1865 514777
or e-mail: info@infideas.com

Where it's at...

235